JOURNEY TO FAMILY

By
KRISTYN ANNE HUIGE

ACKNOWLEDGEMENTS

I would like to thank all of my friends and family for their support and help in the creation of this book. I would especially like to thank my children, Kurdt and Kelly Huige and Sara Huige. Thank you to my grandchildren, Alex, Anthony, Matthew, Dominic, Audra, Natalie, Christina, and Reece. You are all my pride and joy. Thank you for letting me tell your family story.

A special thank you to my sister Corrie and her husband, Chris Burgett, for their very special help and daily phone calls.

I am also grateful for my writing group for their help in composing this book. Linda Kurtz, Joel Thurtell, and Anne Lechartier…I could not have done this work without your help. You made this whole process exciting. Thank you.

Also, thank you to the Osher Lifelong Living Institute (University of Michigan senior activities program) for getting me started during COVID pandemic.

Thank you to neighbors who read, sometimes two versions, of my books: Susan Smereck and Patty and Brian Dillon. Thanks also to good friends who supported me when the going got tough. Elaine Hockman and the ladies' birthday group.

DEDICATION

This book is dedicated to my children, Kurdt and Sara, and to my grandchildren: Alex, Anthony, Matthew, Dominic, Audra, Natalie, Christina and Reece. Thank you for enriching my life.

Table of Contents

PREFACE
JOURNEY TO FAMILY

In 1981, I was a thirty-nine-year-old single psychotherapist who had always longed to have a family. I was born in Belgium at the beginning of World War II. Like many children who grew up during wartime and then emigrated to a different world, I dealt with a good deal of emotional trauma. In my first book, *Escaping a Well of Fear*, I describe my successful struggle to free myself from the past. I had always visualized children in my life, and when I was ready to accept the task of raising kids, I decided to adopt from El Salvador. I chose a foreign adoption because, since I was single, it was the only avenue open for me. I also felt that my past experiences would help me understand the problems my children would be facing. I adopted two children, Kurdt (Francisco), age ll, and Sara (Mirian), age 5. This is our story.

From a strictly selfish perspective, adopting my children was the best experience of my life. I've made many mistakes, learned more than I could have imagined, and have been gifted with the love of two warm, exciting people and eight grandchildren. "Before children," my life was filled with fun, work, learning, and traveling. "After children," my world really opened up. Our time together has been and still is a magnificent journey. There have been valleys and peaks, wonderful times and times I would rather not remember. I have written about the good and the bad. Hopefully, others can learn from my mistakes.

The "ride" I've taken with these two "children" is unlike anything I had anticipated and much more exciting. Everything in my life changed when Sara and Kurdt entered my world. The struggles we experienced and still experience helped solidify our relationship. I decided from day one that we would work out whatever came our way. Most problems have solutions if we look hard enough. There were times when our relationships were strained, and it was hard to be together. Sometimes, when it comes to politics and religion, there are still difficult moments. I feel blessed.

The first two chapters of this book are the pre-adoption stories of my children, as told to me when they were both adults. I thought it was important for you to know the world they came from. They experienced many traumas: some from the war in their home country and some from the cruel, neglectful behaviors of those who were responsible for their care. In 2023, I asked Kurdt if I could interview him for the book. He eagerly accepted my invitation, and we spent hours talking about the horrors he still remembered vividly. We have continued our discussions to this day. Sara and I also spoke of El Salvador, but she was so much younger than her brother, and her memories were limited and hazy.

The remainder of the book consists of stories of our time together. We had our share of struggles, but have resolved most of them. We had many happy times, and we also had our share of pain.

FRANCISCO SALVADOR ALDANA

I would like to tell you something about my life before I was adopted by the Mom I love, Kristyn Huige. My Mom will tell the story of our lives together later. I was adopted when I was almost 12 years old from El Salvador. When I came to the United States, it was like a bomb had gone off in my world; the only familiar person in my life was my little sister, Mirian. All of the people I had loved and felt connected to were gone. Everyone disappeared from my life. There was no one to reach out to. We were alone.

Talk about a dramatic world change. In El Salvador, I was used to roaming about all day…I was my own boss…and I was boss over my brother and sisters. I saw very little of my mother, although she would sometimes leave some money on the table for me to buy food for us. At some point, I'm not sure how old I was, Oscar, my brother, was gone. As he tells the story, he had spilled some milk, and mom kicked him out. He was 5 or 6 years old. What I remember is that he pushed me over a cliff when he was angry and hurt me. My Mom was very angry, and then he disappeared. I didn't know what happened to him. I was supposed to look after him, but he either spilled the milk or hurt me. I felt guilty when he disappeared, but I didn't ask about him. I knew better than to ask questions. I now only had the girls to look after. I would take the money and shop for food, and since there wasn't much money, I had to shop very carefully. I had a job. I looked after the girls. They were my responsibility, and I liked this job. I was independent, and I liked that. There was no one to look after me, and I hadn't needed anyone for years. I was the man in the family.

How did I spend most of my days in El Salvador? I went to school, sometimes, but we had paper but no books. I learned some of the history of my country and I learned to read, but I learned very little math. I didn't go every day, and I can't say that I liked school. The teacher was very critical and would punish us with switches on our hands and back. Mirian and Rosa did not go to school. Nobody looked after them when I wasn't there. At times, when I was not in school, my friends and I played in a huge junk pile near our house. There were all kinds of car stuff and mechanical things, and we enjoyed making things with the junk. I was even able to make some money selling the junk. Sometimes, there were even bodies in this dump, and the garbage pile really smelled terrible. You could smell it all over the neighborhood. I think the people treated us like Lepers because we lived near the garbage pile and even smelled like it.

A lot happened to me and to my family while I was in El Salvador. The war, which had been a part of my life since I could remember, was scary, even for me. When I was around 4 years old, I was caught in a cross-fire, and I was shot in the leg. It really hurt, but I knew that if I went to an adult, I would be severely punished for being wherever I happened to be in order to get hurt. The hole in the front of my leg wasn't too bad, but the back of my leg, where the bullet left my leg, was really big. I wasn't sure what to do. I cried, but decided that would not help me. I went into a store and managed to steal some cotton balls and some bandages. I pushed the cotton balls into the hole in the back of my leg so it would stop bleeding and wrapped it up. I didn't see mom, so I wasn't caught until a few days later when my leg got infected, and boy, did I get it then. Mom beat me up and angrily cleaned my leg. At some point, she took me to the doctor. I told her it wasn't my fault, but she was still angry.

One of the biggest issues for me when I was living in El Salvador was another hurt that took place when I was around 6 years old. In Salvador, no one in the community had a bathroom, and we all shared an out-house behind our shacks. Apparently a woman had been watching me and had a pretty good idea as to when I used the latrine. She pulled me in and made me do stuff to her and she did some things to me. I was scared and hated what she did. She did it several times and warned me not to tell Mom, or she would kill her. I didn't know what to do. After a while, I carefully looked around for her and avoided her. I was faster than she was, and so she didn't get a chance to molest me again. Rosa, my younger sister, remembers our uncle abusing her. Children were not safe.

I also remember that my family moved a lot in Salvador. Things had been better when my father was alive, but he died when I was about 8 years old. After he died, we moved from place to place, sometimes not having a home. Our places were quite a distance apart, so we really didn't get to know our neighbors very well. I remember not having enough food and crawling under my neighbor's house so I could break in and steal food for Mirisn and Rosa. I didn't like stealing, and I worried about getting caught, but we needed food.

After my father died, my mother married a garbage man. He was not a nice guy. He fought constantly with everyone in the family. Mom was often bloody from the beatings. I remember that he had a child with my mother. He beat the baby because it was crying, and it died. I hit him with a stick that had a nail sticking out, and I never saw him again after that.

Strange things happened in our house. One time, I came home when it was already dark. I went into our house and saw a lot of people standing around the table we had in the room. There were candles all over the place, and people were mumbling things I couldn't understand. Suddenly, I saw what they were standing around …it was a small coffin. Shocked, I say: "Rosa". It is Rosa in the coffin! Someone whispers: "Rosa is dead." I can't move, I am so scared. Chanting and mumbling continued for what seemed like hours. Suddenly, Rosa sat bolt upright. People screamed, several left the house, and others were shouting, "Thanks to God." I felt like laughing; the whole scene was so strange. It felt crazy to me. Someone helped Rosa down from the table and she seemed almost normal. It was like she just woke up from a deep sleep. When she saw all of the people and heard the commotion, she started to cry. I went to her and told her she was okay, but I'm really not so sure that she is. She was a bit different after she came back to life, but it's hard to describe what "different" means. I can't forget this scene. It's like it happened yesterday. I still don't understand it. Rosa was different after this. She wandered about, but every chance she got, she started eating dirt. I had to watch her and stop her when I could.

I never felt close to my Mom. She seemed to make no effort to notice me, speak to me, hug me, or even thank me for taking care of the girls. I think she was depressed. I felt alone. I think my whole family was like that. I often wondered why my family didn't look for us after mom was shot by the secret police. We were in an orphanage, and I can't imagine that it would have been hard to find us.

One of my worst memories from El Salvador was when I was walking home from the store. I knew something was wrong at home; I could just tell… so I peeked through some loose boards on the side of the house. I saw several soldiers inside, and they were beating my mother. Suddenly, they shot her, and then they left the house. I don't remember all that happened afterward, but Mirian, Rosa, and I ended up in an orphanage run by nuns. It was not an easy place. We stayed there for what felt like a long time, and then my Mom adopted us. She made a big difference in my life. El Salvador was so violent that I might not have survived childhood.

My life changed completely after Mom adopted us. I was never hungry again. We had a beautiful, very large home on what looked like an estate. I was proud to be living there. I was happy that Sara (Mirian's new name) was with me. We couldn't believe where we were. We had a home. Everything was about to change for us. We were in a wonderful place, but I felt so confused, and I couldn't actually figure out what was real. Were we really safe now? Who was this lady who was now our Mom? Was this all a dream? Would she really let me stay here? Where was Rosa?

This was the world I came from. What will my new life be like? I didn't like my old life in El Salvador. It was hard and lonely. I was hungry most of the time. But it was familiar. I knew what was expected of me. I was my own boss. I knew what this world would provide for me, what it wouldn't, and I knew what I needed to do to survive. Everything changed for my sister and me on May 9, 1981.

MIRIAN DEL CARMEN ALDANA

My memories of El Salvador, my birth country, are hazy and scattered. I was told that I lived with my Mama, two brothers, and my sister. The story I remember is that my brother, Oscar, disappeared one day and never came back to us. Francisco said Mama sent him away because he spilled the milk. He was 5 years old at the time. I was afraid that I would do something terribly wrong and I would get sent away. My big brother, Francisco, looked after us when Mama worked and she worked a lot. What I remember of my house, the last one we lived in together, was that it was made of something like cardboard. It had one window and was very tiny. All of the houses in the neighborhood were close together and were similar in appearance. They looked like they were attached, but they were actually just very close to one another. My house was in a place that smelled very bad. Francisco said it was because of the garbage dump nearby. The dump even had some bodies in it.

I remember feeling sad most of the time. I felt like I was alone a lot, but I do know that Francisco was our boss when Mama was not there. There were, however, many times when Rosa and I were wandering the neighborhood all by ourselves. These were times when both Mama and Francisco were working or when he was in school. We really didn't know what to do when we were alone. If we were lucky, someone would give us some food as we wandered.

Although I have very few memories of my early life, the strongest memory I have is that I heard two men and a woman come into the house. I hid in a cabinet and stayed very quiet. Somehow, I knew that something bad was about to happen. One of them put a gun to her head and pulled the trigger. I saw her die from a hole in the door of the cabinet. She fell down. I held my breath and didn't make a sound or move a muscle. I thought they would kill me if they heard me. I don't know how long I stayed that way. Francisco said that after the people in uniform left, he came into the house. I don't remember anything until the orphanage. I was so confused and sad. I don't really know if I want to remember more.

I remember being in a big building where there were lots of kids and some nuns took me away from Francisco. I screamed and wanted to go home, but they said, "No, you will live here now. Maybe someone will adopt you." I didn't know what they meant by "adopt". Everyone in this place seemed to be crying to be held or fed. It was so noisy and my head hurt. They put me in a crib that had a cover over it with a zipper and kept me there for what felt like most of the time. I cried a lot. I felt like I couldn't breathe. The space seemed so tiny, but they said this would be my bed. I don't really like small spaces. I still don't like small spaces.

When I woke up, I didn't know where I was. I looked for Francisco, my brother, and later in the day, they brought him to me. I don't remember any of this, but he said I hugged him and begged him to take me home. I said: "I want to go home to Mama!"

He said: "She has been shot and is dead. We won't see her anymore. We no longer have a home. We will live here for now. I'll also live here, but I'm with the big kids and can't really come here to see you. You need to stay with the little kids. I'll try to come when I can."

I remember that I cried a lot and felt abandoned. I had a lot of nightmares and I heard bombs and a lot of scary guns. I hated the crib and I didn't want the food. My stomach and my head hurt.

I wanted to go home with my brother, even if my mother wasn't there. After a long time, the people taking care of me told me to sit in a chair. They were going to take my picture and send it to a lady in America who might want to adopt me. I didn't understand what that meant. They told me that if the lady liked the picture that she would take care of me and I would live there. "Would Francisco come too?" The lady said they would take his picture and send it with mine. I didn't know how to look in the picture, but I think I did okay since she adopted both of us.

I hope I don't have a bed like in the orphanage. I wonder what things will be like. Maybe I'll find out what adoption means.

BECOMING FAMILY 1981

"Family…I want a family! I want children. I have always wanted to have children." From the time I was very little, I wanted to be a mother, and yet, as time went on, there were college and graduate schools and then even more schooling towards certifications as a psychotherapist. It was all work for me and no time for fun or frivolous things. I achieved the success I craved and gained acclaim in my chosen profession. I traveled the world as an expert in Transactional Analysis and as a group and family therapist. I was passionate about my work and chosen lifestyle, and yet I wanted more meaning in my life. Work was wonderful, but it was not enough. I had spent a good deal of my life focused on myself, and had spent years in therapy, and I was bored and exhausted with this. There was a layer of life I had not yet explored and that included family. I was tired of ruminating about making a life change. I was ready to do it. I wanted to be there for children in need of a home. I was aware that I also wanted a home and a home meant family for me. Family meant children. I had put my dream of having a family on the back burner for years…I would soon be forty years of age…my time was running out. I would soon be too old to adopt. My journey to family needed to be underway. It was now or never. At the opening of this book you have read the story of the children I chose to adopt. Perhaps I need to give some background with respect to my story.

I was born in Belgium in early 1940, during World War II. The war is part of my story, as I was plagued with post-traumatic shock for a good deal of my life. The trauma of war was exacerbated by many experiences which followed. Emotional issues dominated my life through my teen years and into my mid-twenties. Much of this is described in my book: *Escaping a Well of Fear (Children of World War II)*. After years of psychotherapy, I became successful and was well-known internationally as a therapist and lecturer. I was really enjoying my life. But…I wanted more…I wanted a family. I wanted children.

My work as a Transactional Analyst has been the primary focus of my life. I loved what I was doing. I had organized my practice into time working at home and time doing workshops internationally. My clients in Ann Arbor were very bright, interesting professionals with a broad variety of therapeutic issues. I had set up my home practice to include monthly three-day marathon training and therapy groups, weekly therapy groups and some individual therapy. I preferred all types of group work because sharing issues in group settings gives a great deal of permission to feel, express feelings, and honestly deal with traumatic issues in front of others. With this kind of work, people can learn to accept themselves at very deep levels. In the training groups, I taught professionals usually in the medical or legal fields.

It was clear to me that my lifestyle worked well for a single person with no family; however, I could not imagine all of this travel working for a mom with two children. After adopting my children, I decided I would initially limit my world travel. I had no idea what would follow, but I was prepared to severely curtail travel. I was hoping that the children would get as enthused about travel as I was. Should this not be the case, I was prepared to make whatever adaptations necessary. I was aware that once I reduced the frequency of my global practice, my income would also be reduced. Things would change, some dramatically, but I was ready to take the risks involved.

I decided that I would adopt two children who needed a home. I knew that my job as a parent of older, traumatized children would not be easy, but I nonetheless decided that this is what I would do. Older children are much harder to place than babies, and I felt that with my past experience I would be somewhat better equipped to deal with the many issues that would certainly come up. I decided on two girls, ages three and five. I had a very large house at this time, and I rattled around in it. My four thousand square foot house was in the middle of thirteen wooded acres and I even had a separate twelve hundred square foot office building on the property, perfect for the kind of work I was doing. The big house had five bedrooms and I used only one of them. I wanted this place to become a home, and it needed a family.

I found an adoption agency which dealt with children from El Salvador. A friend had a good experience with this agency, so after several exploratory conversations, I decided to use this group. I applied to adopt two children and very quickly, I was sent the pictures of two children. I fell in love with them at first sight. They were siblings: a boy, Francisco, and a girl, Mirian. They were, however, older than I was prepared for. Francisco was eleven years old and Mirian was five. It was odd, but I really felt that they were already my children. Francisco was small in stature, but he had a strength and pride that told me he was a fighter. He looked protective of his little sister as he stood in front of her. Mirian was also very small for her age and she looked confused and bewildered. She also had the look of a wizened old woman who had been through more than her share of trauma. Both of them looked like they were thinking: "What is going on? What is this all about?"

Francisco was almost twelve and Mirian was almost six. They were much older than the children I had initially planned on adopting. They were both very undernourished, with shocks of beautiful black hair and dark eyes. They were beautiful. They were half-brother and sister and both had experienced wartime violence and witnessed the shooting death of their mother. Francisco's father had died several years earlier and Mirian's father was nowhere to be found. Many months later, I discovered that they had two other siblings I had not known about, Rosa and Oscar. I thought about the ages of my children. I was aware that the older a child is when adopted, the more unknown and often painful traumas he/she may have suffered. Francisco had experienced a civil war, had lost his father, and had seen his mother murdered, and this is only the information I was able to find out. Based on my own experience, I knew that much more happens to children than what is reported during wartimes. This would be no cake-walk. I had my work cut out for me. Was I ready for this experience? Were they ready for the new life I was offering them? Will I be in over my head? I've been in over my head before, and I succeeded. Well…here I go.

I was aware that many foreign adoptions of children, especially older children, have devastating outcomes. In fact, several years earlier, I had begun a research project exploring success and failure in foreign adoptions. I interviewed people who had adopted children from Romania, Russia and China. They told stories of violence and feared for their own safety. I was aware that with some children, early psychological damage was severe, and chances that they could bond with new families were bleak. The adoptive parents were given little or no information about the past experiences of their child, so they felt totally unprepared when they were met with the child's rage, fear, lack of control, unusual repetitive behaviors, inability to bond and other very stressful situations. Some of the parents were so frightened of their children's increased rage as they got older and bigger and stronger that they returned them to state custody. I knew that my children would be considered hard to place, but I felt that I was perhaps more capable of dealing with their issues than most adoptive parents. Was I kidding myself?

What would I do if my children were plagued with intense rage…even homicidal rage? Older adopted children are often terrified of closeness, as they experienced very little in their early years. For some, closeness did not bring warmth and comfort, but pain and fear. Living in a nuclear family brings closeness. Would they be able to tolerate family life? I decided that I would assume that all of the above issues were possible. If these issues are present, I will deal with them to the best of my ability, but once we become a family, there is no going back. Would I be ready to forgive myself when I made mistakes in this process and move on? I needed to let myself know that I WOULD make mistakes and YES, I am prepared to forgive myself. Also…this is a forever deal. I needed to stay mindful of the fact that this would be a slow process and that patience was the key. Truth telling and forgiveness also play roles in this process. Children don't get over trauma with just a change of scenery. I knew there would be a great deal of testing limits, of moving forward and then retreating. I was also aware that many of the issues I had worked on for years were not totally resolved, and would enter into the mix and either hinder or help resolve problems. Yes…I was sure that they would. Would I be ready to get the outside help I might need? Yes…I would. So we would be three "damaged" people working life out together... feeling our strengths and accepting our weaknesses.

In less than six months, I completed the paperwork and passed the home study needed to adopt. I'm sure that the fact that I made a good income influenced the speed with which everything was accomplished. I could not, however, believe the speed at which this whole process traveled. The children arrived on Mother's Day, 1981. I could not go to El Salvador to get them because the war had gotten worse and four nuns from the orphanage had just been killed. So, there was even more sadness and stress for my children to deal with.

A FIRST PLANE TRIP MEMORIES 5-9-81 (FRANCISCO)

Who is this woman taking Mirian and me to the airport? Where are we going? I was told Michigan, but what is that? Where is that? Are we safe with these people? I need to look after Mirian. Are the other kids who are traveling with us going to the same place?

We get on the airplane. I've never been on a plane before. I'm holding Mirian's hand and we sit down next to each other. Our hands are wet with fear. Where are we going? Adoption…what is it? The lady taking us seems to think that we should be so happy about this. I don't really understand her. We seem to be going from one bad place to another. What makes her think that this is something to be so happy about? And…where is Rosa? Mom had told me to look after both of the girls. Mirian's afraid so I tell her that I am here and that all will be good. She's also afraid of the plane. I am, too, but I don't tell her that. I tell her to go to sleep and the trip won't take long. I lied…it took a very long time.

When we land, we are all very tired. It's night and we are taken to a house, given some food, and we go to sleep. I'm told that my new mom will be here in the morning to take us to a new home. I wonder why she didn't come to get us. I want this trip to be over.

I wake up and there's another strange woman in the room. She has lots of blond curly hair and green eyes. She is tall and looks very happy. I think that she's telling me that she is my new Mom. There's also another lady with her who is speaking Spanish, but I don't really understand her. I feel so tired and confused. Mirian's still sleeping.

I should wake her up, so I touch her shoulder. She says she's tired, but she gets up and the lady…the one who says she's our Mom…gives us some new clothes to put on. She helps Mirian dress. Our clothes are big for us…but they are new. I haven't had new clothes before. We need to give the clothes we wore while traveling back to the orphanage…the lady who brought us told me that. The new shoes Mom brought with her are way too big, so she asks the lady in charge if we can keep the ones we wore to travel. She says okay.

Mom starts to talk to the lady that brought us on the plane. Mirian and I walk around and find the car she came in. It's a beautiful yellow Mercedes. I love it. This is the first time I felt happy today. We stand next to the car and wait. Shortly, our Mom and the travel lady come rushing out. They were worried that we had disappeared. No one noticed us before when we did our own thing and disappeared. It is also weird having to have everything that we say or they say…translated. It's hard to talk.

I'm so confused. There's no one who can explain things to me so I can tell Mirian. The lady with our Mom, who speaks Spanish, doesn't speak my language. I can understand a word here or there, but not much.

Where are we going? I'm sitting in the front seat. It's a beautiful car. I think it belongs to my new Mom. Boy…it feels odd saying that. They gave me a box with some small toys…cars and stuff. I've seen some before, but I've never had any toys before and they are brand new. I'm not sure what to do with them. I wonder if they are mine to keep.

I'm feeling angry because no one has told me anything about Rosa. The lady on the plane had no idea what I was talking about.

She didn't know I had another sister and a brother. She said, "Oh, she'll turn up somewhere." I felt like crying with this statement. I keep wondering where she is. Why can't she be with us? I'm supposed to look after both of the girls. I haven't seen her for a while, but when we were in the same orphanage, at least I knew where she was even if I didn't see her. Now, I'm too far away to find her.

I fall asleep, but as I'm drifting off I hear Mirian singing and chirping in the back seat. I'm happy she's having such a good time with the lady…Mom. I'm not as worried. I fall asleep and when I wake up, we're in a large city. We're not at our home yet. It's so strange not being able to say what I'm thinking. What will we do if we can't talk to one another?

After a while we pull into a long drive surrounded by huge trees. There's a big house and a small house and even a lake. Wow! Where are we? Is this going to be our home? Oh my gosh…there are two big dogs. Will they hurt me? When the car stops, I open the door and the dogs want to come into the car. They are licking and hopping on me. I think they like me. Wow…will we also have dogs to play with? I wonder how many people live in this house. Is it like the orphanage with a lot of people? Does the Spanish-speaking lady also live here?

Mom takes us into the house and it is beautiful. I can't believe we're going to live here. I'd been so worried that we were going to another awful place and look at this. The kitchen is amazing and has lots of food. I've never seen a kitchen like this. The dogs also come into the house. I can't believe this place. Mom shows us our rooms. We each have a room of our own. We don't have to share. Our rooms have beds and toys.

MIRIAN'S MEMORIES 5-9-1981

I've got a doll. I've never had a doll. Mom gives me a wonderful stuffed animal. He's light brown and very soft and cuddly. I have new clothes. I don't know where I am or where I'm going, but Francisco says everything is good and I shouldn't worry. I like the lady …our Mom. I'm glad that Francisco is here. I wonder where we are going. This is a nice car. I've never been in a nice car. In fact, I've never been in a car. I wish I knew what people were saying. I don't understand them. I know some songs, maybe Mom will sing them with me. Everything is so different here. There is nothing familiar to me. It's really confusing. I'm scared that I won't be able to say what I need. I'm glad the lady knows the word "banyo," and she took me to one and helped me.

I'm really tired and fall asleep. When I woke up, we were at a very large house surrounded by trees. Oh my goodness, there were two big dogs trying to get into the car when Chico (Francisco) opened the door of the car. They're so big that they're a bit scary. I like the older one, Rusty, best. My Mom shows us into the house and it is so beautiful. I can't believe I am going to live here. At least, I think this is going to be my home. Mom says we each have a bedroom and she shows us. My room is wonderful, it has a very big bed and lots of toys and even clothes. Chico also has a big room of his own. We've never had toys before. I don't know what to touch first.

KRISTYN HUIGE'S MEMORIES DAY 1 5-9-1981

The drive to Cleveland to pick up my children began before 5 AM on Mother's Day in 1981. I asked a friend to drive with me from Ann Arbor as I didn't want to be distracted from the kids on my way home. I was anxious, and it was great to have a friend with me. We made good time and got to our destination very early. We waited for a bit, but by 6:30 A.M., I was ready to knock on the door. An adult, the director of the agency, answered the door and invited us in. "I know how anxious you must feel," she said as she led us into a small bedroom where I saw two small children sleeping. The older child, a boy, stretched and opened his eyes. He spoke to the woman and she told him that I was his "Mama." He looked happy and woke his little sister and told her who I was. I didn't understand much of what was said, but I loved the smiles. I took out the clothes I had brought for the kids, gave Francisco his tracksuit, and helped Mirian dress. They both seemed sleepy and confused, but happy with the new clothes.

I wondered to myself how we would manage to communicate since I did not understand what they said... I had learned some Spanish, but this didn't resemble what I had been learning. I was relieved that I had hired someone at home who taught Spanish to help us with this problem. I decided we would do fine. I'd been through learning a different language myself and I survived. It was important, however, to remind myself of the frustrations everyone involved would experience.

The agency director and I exchanged paperwork and chatted for a few minutes. We looked for the kids throughout the house but they were nowhere to be found. I thought, "You've got to be kidding…I lost my kids within an hour of meeting them." Luckily, we found them standing by my car, ready to move on. I gave Francisco some small toys in a box. He looked confused but took the box and held onto it very securely. I gave Mirian a doll and she was thrilled. Francisco rode in the front of the car with my friend and I rode in the back with Mirian. He was very quiet and barely moved a muscle. I buckled him into the seat and I don't think he had seen seatbelts before. Throughout the trip, Francisco was absolutely quiet. Mirian, however, was quite animated. She bounced in her seat, sang songs and laughed.

I wondered what was going on in their heads. Here I was, a stranger, and they were off into the unknown with me. I couldn't even reassure them that they would be okay. They loved my car, and it seemed to provide the reassurance I couldn't.

I have driven to Cleveland before, but the return trip never seemed so long. I wonder what is going on in Francisco's mind. I wish I could talk to him and reassure him. I wish I knew what he was thinking. I'm glad that both kids fell asleep for at least part of our trip.

Finally…this is the longest day I can remember ... .We arrived home. The kids seem very excited about the house and the yard. Suddenly, we're surprised by my dogs, two very large golden retrievers. At first, the kids are afraid, but the dogs are soon on them, kissing and loving them. Language was not a problem here…all it took was a full frontal assault and many kisses. Both children seem to love dogs. Everybody is talking loudly and fast. The kids understand each other and my friend and I understand one another. We all seem to understand our feelings and at this point, we all seem happy. Words and their meanings seem unimportant.

We enter the house and the children look absolutely amazed. Looks of incredulity and joy…and when they see their bedrooms, I hear shrieks of joy. They go back and forth from one room to another. The bedrooms are set up for a girl and a boy. The rooms are equipped with toys, clothes and furniture. They rush from one room to another, showing one another toys and clothing. I have no idea as to what they are thinking or feeling. I can only guess that all is well based on facial expressions and the tenor of the shouts. What fun they seem to be having.

I know I am going to have my work cut out for me if I am to understand what is going on with the children. I wish I could understand what they are saying. From my own experience with learning a new language, it took about two months before I was able to grasp some of what was being said to me. What I needed to do now was find ways we could laugh together and create some of the bonds that lead to family.

BECOMING FAMILY

Our first few weeks were a wonderful honeymoon time. Everybody was happy, cooperative, and basically "over the moon" with our new family group. Everything was new for the children. The social worker I was working with suggested naming the kids…basically giving them new names. I was hesitant, but decided to go along with this. I spoke to the children about "American names," and they were excited about changing their names. Mirian loved her new name of "Sara," and Francisco did not like the name "Matthew." I told him to take his time and think about what name he would like. In the meantime, he went by Chico, Cisco or Pancho….all names he had been called in El Salvador. He apparently had seldom been called Francisco. I was following the advice of the worker who said that changing names was a good idea and would help them integrate into American culture as well as avert teasing. I had chosen to change my name as an adult (from Wilfrida Ferdinanda Huige to Kristyn Huige) because I felt my name had been a problem for me as a child. I had been bullied and teased about my name and I had always felt different from my peers. My concern about changing the children's names was that this had not been their choice, even though they were given a chance to reject the whole idea. I had been an adult and the idea and choice were mine. It was more than a year before my son came up with the name he wanted: Kurdt Salvador Huige, after the lead singer in a heavy metal band. The name really fit him and he has been happy with it. The children will be referred to as Sara and Kurdt for the duration of this book. I dwelled on this for a long time, and finally decided for myself that this was the wrong thing to do. The only parts of El Salvador the children were able to bring with them were the shoes on their feet and their names. In retrospect, I feel bad that I had them change names and would not recommend this to anyone.

During those first weeks, it appeared that Sara was consistently experiencing the newness of her world. Everything was totally new to her. She marveled at the door to her room, the door knob, pens, pencils, crayons, paper, books, videos, etc. She loved the clothes I had bought her and changed clothes a number of times per day. In fact, sometimes five or six times. She and Kurdt both loved having their own rooms, but Sara was reluctant to use it at night. I'm sure that she had never slept alone and that this was a frightening experience for her. She initially slept with me in my bed and seemed to like that. The house and the property and the "things" in the house were overwhelming to both kids at first.

In the daytime, both Sara and Kurdt began the day in their own rooms, frequently running back and forth to one another's rooms. I was amazed at how tidy the kids kept their rooms. Everything was neatly organized and in place…even their beds were made. I realized that if I wanted this behavior to continue, I would need to clean up my act. Both of them were eager to learn. Sara was affectionate and craved physical contact. Kurdt was more reticent about sharing and about physical contact, such as hugs. They both became aware that free expression was allowed in their new home. They no longer held their faces and their bodies as rigidly as they had. Our lives became a giant game of pantomime. Every day was a new experience.

I invited some of the neighborhood boys and girls to the house to meet the children. Kurdt very quickly developed friendships with the boys, while Sara played with the girls but kept her distance. She seemed more interested in relating with me; in fact, she became a bit possessive of me. The group of six boys, all around Kurdt's age, laid claim to the basement and to the outdoors. The noise level in the house kicked up a number of notches. I loved it.

Communication was definitely a frustrating problem. I had hired a Spanish teacher to help us communicate; however, when the children first arrived, he said he did not understand the "Spanish" they were speaking. He thought it was some dialect or perhaps an indigenous language, but he felt he could not help me. So it was up to me. We did a lot of guessing about what we wanted to say. We learned pantomime, some Spanish, and worked hard on English. I thought that what was important was that we find some way to develop a bond, to relate in some non-verbal way…perhaps to laugh together. Aha! I know what will work.

In the early evenings, when we were alone after dinner, the kids and I gathered around the TV in the family room and plopped ourselves onto some giant bean bags to watch silent movies. We fell in love with Charlie Chaplin, the Three Stooges, Laurel and Hardy, Shirley Temple, and a host of other stars from the silent movies. I chose these movies because I loved them and wanted to find things we could laugh about together. For these movies, we did not need language. We didn't need a deep intellect. We just needed to know how to see the world and laugh. We were on the same plane when it came to slapstick comedy in movies that did not rely on words. We laughed and laughed and also ate ourselves silly with popcorn. We did not need language to have fun together and we really got to know each other in an intense way. Sara loved to snuggle at this time, and Kurdt was still young enough to be part of a people pile. Our relationships became much more relaxed. I believe that a family that laughs together can work out most things that come up, if not everything. As the weeks rolled on, we added to our list of favorites with the Beatles, Michael Jackson, cartoons and for Kurdt, high-action movies. With the cartoons came stories with words and between the TV, local friends, and my efforts with language, we were beginning to really understand one another with words as well as actions. Once school began for both kids, we were out of the woods when it came to English. At home, we were doing great when it came to understanding one another, but language was an issue at school.

In watching the kids experiencing the same dramatic changes I had gone through as a child, I knew what it was like to move to a different language and the horrible frustration of being unable to say what you want or feel. I believe that my early experiences helped me clarify some of these issues for the kids. I understood the significance of having familiar smells, sights, sounds and even foods. I didn't know what would be familiar to the children as I had never been in El Salvador. When I fixed Mexican food, it wasn't Salvadoran. It smelled and tasted different. Kurdt kept asking for carne asada and no one seemed to have any idea what food this was. I figured out that it was a type of beef, but I had no idea how to prepare or what spices to use. Now, Ann Arbor has a Salvadoran restaurant, but then, nothing.

Cultural differences were apparent fairly early in our time together. One incident that stands out for me was Kurdt's reaction to his new bike. I had purchased a bike with large tires, specifically built for rough terrain and for racing. It was a beauty! It was a lovely blue. Kurdt was ecstatic and learned how to ride it fairly quickly, since he didn't worry about falling off. I went outside to see how he was doing, only to discover that he had taken my oil paints and was painting his vehicle a variety of bright colors. My first reaction was horror. I said nothing and thought to myself that I needed to control both my face and my tongue. I said nothing, but turned, hopefully before Kurdt saw me. I needed to get control of myself. I acted like I had forgotten something inside the house and momentarily fled the scene. I asked myself why he would deliberately destroy this wonderful bike. At some point, when I came to my senses, I remembered that in Mexico and Central American countries, bright colors decorate almost everything. Kurdt was simply making this bike his own. He was putting his mark on it. When I had gathered my resources, felt in control of myself, and thought about what I would say, I opened the door and stepped onto the patio.

"Wow, look at you…painting your new bike. It's going to be the talk of your friends." I spoke hesitantly, but I did have a "smile" on my face. Kurdt looked up at me and smiled broadly. He said: "I like it. I'm making it beautiful." He seemed so incredibly happy. He was truly making this bike his own and bringing his culture into the scene. I'm glad I was able to control myself and not give vent to the first thing that crossed my mind.

Our first few weeks were filled with many different activities. We had doctor visits where I learned that both children were severely malnourished. The doctor recommended a nutritional drink, but neither child would drink it, so rather than struggle over this issue, I made nutritious meals which they devoured and loved. I thought it might take them longer to catch up growthwise, but they would catch up.

Everything was new to the kids. They had never been in a kitchen with so many magical things in it. The pantry was particularly amazing to Sara as she would open up different sections and would find food in all of them. They had not experienced indoor toilets, running water, bathtubs with warm water, bubble baths, pajamas, doors with handles, fireplaces, and all the food imaginable. I heard one squeal of delight after another. I loved showing how everything worked. I was charmed by their expressions of delight and the look of awe on their faces.

VISITORS

We had many visitors during the first few weeks and months. My Mom came to visit and to help, and she was definitely helpful. She was firm but loving. The kids loved her, and she could really get them to listen to her and obey what she said. I was secretly hoping that Mom would stay much longer…maybe even that she would move in, but she was probably finished with raising children. I was concerned that Kurdt was picking on Sara and I wanted him to stop. Mom said that Sara was crafty and would often set Kurdt up to look like the "bad guy", and then she could play the victim. And here, I thought I was the expert when it came to psychological games. I was often in the habit of trying to make everything right for everyone, and that was usually not possible. Mom wasn't worried about that, she was quite good at making kids solve whatever problem they were dealing with.

My sister, Corrie, also came to visit and the kids loved her. They played all kinds of games on the patio, and while playing, Corrie and I enjoyed a relaxing glass of wine. I don't know how we did it, but we communicated LOVE and everyone got the message. Strangely, it never crossed my mind that Corrie would not feel as ecstatic about the adoption as I did. She later told me that she was panicked that there would be no room for her in my life. She was really afraid of losing me. We had always been very close and I had felt that nothing could come between us. I was surprised that Corrie thought children would change that. The reality is that children did affect the intimacy of that relationship. I wondered if other friends or family felt the same way.

Other visitors during week one included Oz and Pearl from India, friends and trainees of mine who came for some supervision of their work and to visit. They were incredibly helpful for an issue I had no experience with: lice. The kids had complained about itching and were scratching their heads. I got them haircuts, but didn't know what I should look for on their heads.

Pearl said, "Let me take a look; we deal with itchy heads all the time in India. Ah…just as I thought, the kids have lice."

"Wow…I'll go and get some of the shampoo people use for lice. I've never seen this before…what do I need to look for in their heads?"

"Here, you can see the nits on the shaft of the hair. The solution is quick and we can do it as soon as you get the shampoo we need."

After rushing to the store, I managed to bring what we needed and then the two experts on lice (Oz and Pearl) took over and got the kids laughing and jumping around as they washed the infested heads. We had an evening of laundry (clothes and sheets) as well as heads. Even though we worked all afternoon and evening on the lice project, we all had a good time. I took a lot of pictures and everyone had a good laugh.

Other early visitors included Om Jac and Tante Molly. I loved both of them so much and really appreciated their visit. They said they came from the Netherlands to support the kids and myself. The children were getting a good sense of a supportive family and friends and seemed to love all of our visitors. The visitors grew to love the kids and provided a good deal of support which I was aware I needed. The kids loved the Dutch cooking and marveled at how tall

Om Jac was. They were also fascinated that there was another language to deal with…Dutch.

Mom stayed about a month, and in that time, Sara had all of her teeth surgically removed. They were tiny black stubs and her whole mouth was badly infected. I was grateful that Mom was still at the house as she could be with Kurdt while I was with Sara at the hospital. I tried to explain to Sara what was going to happen to her; however, I could only do the minimum with only pantomime at my disposal. How do you tell a little girl who doesn't understand your language that all of her teeth need to be pulled? I got her to the hospital and all was well until we got to the surgical suite. I was able to accompany her to this point, and when I was about to leave, she started screaming and hanging onto me. The medical staff tried to take her from me. I suggested that they move away and let me calm her down. I got her onto the table and in a hospital gown, but she knew something was up and wouldn't even sit down.

"Are you going to sedate her?" I asked the nurse next to me.

"Yes," she said. "Here's the cone. See if you can put it over her nose."

Sara and I played with the cone until she sat down and seemed sleepy. I was starting to get sleepy myself, so I handed my little girl and everything else over to the nurse and the operation proceeded. Sara did very well post-surgery. Her mouth had apparently been causing her a considerable amount of pain and she happily let us know the pain was gone. We went home to grandma and she introduced Sara to popsicles which was a wonderful discovery. Grandma asked if her mouth hurt and Sara said, "a little." Within a very short time, new teeth started breaking through her gums. They were white and beautiful and her mouth no longer hurt her. The doctor said that the infections in her mouth, if left untreated, could have killed her. I was grateful that we could deal with these physical issues and that Sara was cooperative, even though she did not understand what was going on.

Mom loved the children and was great with them. She did, however, seem more tired than the Mom I remembered. I would have loved asking her to stay, but I thought she had done her share of raising kids. I later found out that she worried that I might ask her, because she knew she was too tired to take on another family.

SARA THE SCREAMER

While I loved the visitors, I was looking forward to time alone with my children. A word of caution: be careful what you wish for. We were finally alone, and the first evening, Sara initiated what I thought was "testing the limits." When I put her to bed at 8 pm, the usual time, she started screaming at the top of her lungs. I had no idea what was going on. I didn't know what she wanted, or if she was hurting, or what was happening. All I could do was hold her, walk with her and rock her. I even sang to her. She seemed to like the singing, but didn't stop crying. I felt overwhelmed, but after about 3 hours, she fell asleep. This continued each night and yet, during the day, she was the happiest creature you have ever seen. I was getting frustrated when the screaming didn't seem to have an ending. I would have done anything to stop the wailing. I was concerned, however, that if I focused on stopping the screaming, she might repress pain that would be better expressed now. Was a part of her trying to work out earlier traumas? I had no idea as to what was going on below the surface of the screaming. Usually, after 3 hours, she would fall asleep…I was grateful for this. The sad part was that even after weeks of this, I felt we were no further in trying to figure out what this was all about. What did the screaming mean to Sara? Kurdt, in the meantime, was panicked. He worried that it would all be too much for me and that I would give up on both of them. I tried to reassure him, but I don't think he believed me.

I started to question myself as to my abilities when it comes to parenting. I had dreamed that I would have the answers to the problems that would come up, and that I would just know what to do. I had to work hard to ground myself in reality. I had a limited frame of reference for all of this painful screaming and crying. I did not know where this pain came from or what it meant. I could guess…but I had no sense of certainty. I had very little information about the children's history. Kurdt said she had done a good deal of screaming at the orphanage, but he only heard about it from the women helping…he hadn't heard it himself. As Kurdt's English improved, he was able to tell me more about the orphanage experience. She had slept with the adult women because she screamed so much. She was kept in a crib with a plastic cover that was zipped shut when she was in bed. The power of the screaming was starting to wear me down.

I'm not sure how long the screaming went on, but it felt like forever. It was probably around a month. I wondered if making all of this noise was actually helpful to Sara. It certainly didn't help either Kurdt or myself. I again asked her, "What do you want? What do you need?" Then, the screaming began to paint a picture for me. She started screaming, "TV…TV…TV…etc." Now, I felt I had something to go with. Suddenly it felt more OK to find a way to put a stop to all of this noise.

By now, I was a nervous wreck. I wondered what I had gotten myself into. I reminded myself that I was in for the duration. I considered all of the information I had about what was going on and decided I would know what to do. If I was going to be successful with Sara I would need to use my support system to help me win this battle with my little girl.

I asked several friends to come for a weekend and help me out with this issue. I needed them to hold my hands and keep me from rescuing Sara. She had let me know that she wanted to stay up as late as her brother, and I said: "NO, you're too young. No TV at night." She started screaming…I left the room. I didn't hold her or cuddle her. I was not angry…I just left the room. Her screaming continued for several hours, but when we watched her through the window on the patio, she was sitting upright, turning the pages of a magazine…all the while screaming. That did not look like a kid in distress to me. Night one passed. Night two was similar to night one, but the screaming took less time and she fell asleep on her own. Night three was different. I went into the bedroom and asked her how the screaming was going.

"Good," she said.

"How much longer do you need to scream?" I wasn't sure I had asked this question since I used a combination of gestures and broken Spanish.

"A little more," was her answer.

The next day, she didn't initiate the screaming. She came to me and made the motions for tears and for "no." I asked her if she was finished.

"Done…Finished," she said. And she was done. The screaming at night was over.

I survived the first battle with this very strong-willed child. I think I succeeded in this first parenting dilemma, but I wasn't sure. I wasn't even sure what had happened. I had no idea as to the battles ahead and I have to admit that I'm grateful for that.

Since Sara's screaming time, she has done wonderfully at bedtime. We've established our own evening ritual which consists of washing up, brushing teeth, some play time and then a book and some music. After that we have the usual requests for water and lots of kisses.

Screaming is still an occasional part of our lives. Sara will occasionally scream when I go down to the office. Her fear of abandonment is still strong. She wants to hold onto me and is reluctant to let go. It will take time for her to deal with this fear.

UNIFORMS AND POLICE

At the beginning of our second month together, I began to realize that the children seemed terrified of anyone in a uniform, especially the police. This was a problem, because if they needed help and I wasn't around, they needed to get help from people in uniform. While driving to the grocery, I observed a traffic accident and stopped to help. The car that was hit by a truck happened to be a police patrol car. No one was hurt, but the young policeman was grateful that I was willing to be a witness for him. He said if there was anything he could do, he would be happy to help me. I told him about the children and their fear of the police. I asked if he could drop by the house in an official car and get to know them and possibly reduce their anxiety. He was very willing to do so and later that day, a police car drove into our drive.

Kurdt saw the car and panicked. He grabbed Sara's hand and dragged her into the house and wanted me to go with him. He kept yelling, "Police…Police"! When I said "no," he pulled Sara into the bathroom and locked the door. I told him that the policeman was my friend.

"Police…amigo…amigo." I spoke hesitantly but loudly.

The policeman and I talked to the kids through the door and slowly, Kurdt opened up. We all went out to the police car, and the kids got to sit in the car, play with the siren and the lights and have a wonderful time. They wore their friend's police hat and pretended to be policemen themselves. They had a great time. Most of the interactions were pantomime but I think everyone understood.

As an adult, Kurdt has spoken of this time. Police had been the people who had killed his mother and had made life painful for everyone. He had always been afraid of uniforms and had done his best to avoid anyone in uniform. When he first saw this deputy, he was terrified. He worried that I would get killed and that we would all die. On first arriving at our house, Kurdt thought he would never again have to see a policeman or even someone in uniform. It was really a shock when this sheriff's deputy arrived on our doorstep. Kurdt remembers this experience as initially frightening but he was happy that it ended up being a lot of fun. He was so glad that this policeman and I had taken the time to help rid him of this fear. He said that he felt better about the police in America, but he wasn't sure about "all of them." I thought it was probably wise for him to remain a bit guarded.

Day 1 Sara, Kurdt

Our House

Day 2

Police are Ok

Corrie visits

Oom Jac Tante molly

Grandma visits

A Red Bird

Kurdt (aka. Chico, Cisco, or Pancho)

The neighborhood on Valentine Road was a paradise for Kurdt and his buddies. They formed very solid and strong friendships, some of which last to this day. This world was heaven on earth as they biked all over, played games, made movies, watched movies, spent overnights together and snacked on everything available in the groups' homes or Derrick's barn. Later, some of these kids formed a rock band, with Kurdt on drums and guitar. This neighborhood gang provided a safety zone for Kurdt as he could feel he really belonged and was fully accepted. At the same time, he could still set an emotional distance that made the world less overwhelming. They were all good kids and on the whole, accepted one another's issues and idiosyncrasies without using them in power games. It was OK if you or your family were a little different and no fuss was made about this.

Intimate family relationships were more of an issue and took a good deal of work on all of our parts. As we got to know each other better, the emotional distance between us grew smaller and thus more frightening for a child who did not want to get close. I believe that Kurdt had made many early decisions that, in order to feel safe, he had to maintain distance, and that was getting more and more difficult for him as time went on. I still knew very little of his early life or his life in El Salvador as he seldom spoke of this "before time." I was basically drawing conclusions based on our lives together. Overnights with friends were activities that were very normal for a boy his age and helped a youngster deal with anxiety related to closeness in the family. It's a safety valve, and I know it to be helpful. I also wanted to strengthen our family ties and do more activities at home. I set some limits on overnights even though I understood their value. I felt he was too young to emotionally exit the home in favor of the neighborhood.

Kurdt's best friend was Derrick, and Derrick's family really extended their hospitality to him. He spent many overnights there, and he and Derrick also enjoyed spending time in their barn. Both boys had bikes and enjoyed racing them. Kurdt had a bike that was built for racing, and when I purchased it, I was told the frame had a lifetime warranty. Within 6 months, Kurdt broke the frame and just as the warranty said, the bike was replaced at no cost. Kurdt was dumbfounded. He was shocked that another bike was there for him… "What a strange world." Again, the new bike had a warranty and again, within 6 months, the frame was broken. At this point, I was quite suspicious. How could this happen? I followed the boys as they took off for riding in the neighborhood. I was horrified when I saw that they were racing their bikes off a cliff into the lake. I'm grateful that no one was hurt, but Kurdt again broke the bike frame. I felt like giving them all a paddling for having been so stupid. Kurdt was apparently the wildest of the crew and willingly did any dares that came his way. I told all of the boys that this needed to stop. It was as though someone had taken their favorite toy away, however, all agreed to find something else to do. After this third bike was destroyed, I told Kurdt that he needed to earn his next bike…I had many chores he could do. In the meantime, I chose a beautiful bike for myself to replace his broken one. When I ordered my bike, the shop owner laughed and said he was grateful but he added that the bike company wanted to hire Kurdt to test their bikes. I said, "No thanks, I'm afraid he'd get hurt." Kurdt was much more careful with the bike he was able to purchase with his own funds.

HONEYMOON?

I had been dealing with one issue after another, but I was grateful that so far, the problems all seemed manageable…well…Sara's nighttime screaming was on the verge of being unmanageable, but that seemed solved at this point. I reminded myself that this was supposed to be the honeymoon period, where everyone was on their best behavior. I don't think that we all got the message, but we were doing well. Both children were adjusting to their new world and seemed quite happy…most of the time. After taking several months off of work to acclimate to family life, I was ready to resume my therapy practice on a limited basis. I was prepared to work with two groups per week…a total of nine hours away from the house. My office was down the hill from the house…in other words…close by.

Going down to the office quickly became problematic as I had to tear a screaming Sara away from me and leave her with our housekeeper, Lorene. This was also an issue when it came to going to the grocery store or separating from Sara in any way. I tried to comfort her and reassured her that I would be back soon. I could understand the panic she was feeling. She had been through so much and every day in her new home seemed to bring new changes. I knew, though, that she needed to get used to being separated from me. She also needed to learn that I would return to her and that our relationship would not change during our time away from each other. I would be her mother when I left to go to work and I would be her mother when I came home to be with her and Kurdt. I remained calm and talked to her briefly. Her English was still not strong, but her new language was beginning to make some sense to her. I encouraged Lorene to distract Sara with various activities. I knew that this separation anxiety would take time to deal with. She had lost so many people and I assumed that when people left her immediate vision, Sara never knew whether it would be forever. In fact, often, it was forever. They never returned. We developed a ritual about going away. I reminded her that each time after I had left, I came back. She really needed to believe I would come back. Slowly, she began to believe.

Kurdt, in the meantime, took something of a back seat. It must have been incredibly hard for him to compete with this beautiful, emotional five-year-old sister. At times, he appeared really angry with her and even threatened her, and at other times, especially when she was crying, he was upset by her sadness. He seldom shared any sadness of his own, but he was clearly moved by hers and would have done anything to see her happy. He appeared very jealous of her at times and would even say that she was not his sister. He continued to be frightened that if Sara was a big problem that I would give up on them. I constantly reassured him that we would work through all of these issues and that we would stay together. This was his home and I was his Mom.

When we went places in the car, our usual form of communication, gestures, pantomime, and making faces, was not available as I needed to look at the road. One godsend for me was that I had a giant collection of Beatles tapes. Kurdt became an ardent fan and played them incessantly. Luckily, I also loved the music. From then on, everywhere we went, we would play the Beatles music and sing along to it at the top of our lungs. I was grateful that the three of us found such a joyous way of breaking the silence. Singing was our way of being together, and it felt wonderful. We did not need words.

Kurdt was an angel through the summer months of that first year, but then very little was asked of him and all he seemed to do was play. It's hard to discipline or even to explain chores or set limits without language. Later in the summer, I hired tutors to see where the kids were academically and to get them used to school work. Kurdt complained loudly and most definitely saw them as infringing on his personal space. He was used to having his own way and when I questioned something he wanted to do, he became very upset, withdrew, and refused to speak. Working with the tutors was difficult, but we did it, and I learned that Sara would start with Kindergarten or grade 1 and Kurdt was way behind grade level, but he could catch up with work.

Once, Mark, a neighborhood friend, invited him to go to a baseball game. I asked if it was alright with Mark's father, and Kurdt apparently misunderstood me. He withdrew and refused to say anything and stood in a corner for the longest time. I had to work, so I called Mark's parents and asked them if they would come and pick Kurdt up for the game. I explained that he had put himself in the corner and needed help to get out. I was clear that Kurdt could go but that he had misunderstood me and they would need to talk him out of the corner. I told an unlistening Kurdt he could go to the game. I even wrote his permission out for him and taped it to the wood trim in the corner where he stood. I had written a big "OKAY to GO." When they arrived, everybody in the house plus Mark's parents and Mark had to convince Kurdt that it was okay to go to the game. It was almost as though he would hear one word of a sentence or a well-scrutinized intonation and decide that there was no way he would get what he wanted or needed. He was definitely used to not getting what he wanted. A long time ago he decided that he would have to fight hard to get his needs met.

What was fascinating about the whole limit testing situation with the children was that Kurdt waited until Sara had "finished" before he began his testing. They never seemed to present problems at the same time…which was a blessing. Kurdt reacted powerfully whenever I said the word "no ". As a result, I found myself holding back when it came to saying "no" about particular events. I kept telling myself that when our language improved that I would be in a better position to say "no," and to explain what that particular situation might be. Waiting was a mistake. Hindsight being so clear, I probably would have done well to have looked into Kurdt's behavior patterns. Doing so, I probably would have seen a direct connection between lack of sleep and nasty behavior the following day. I would have had to say "no" to TV watching and would have sent Kurdt to bed earlier. I don't want to oversimplify. There were many situations which resulted in negative, snarky and rebellious behavior. I needed to find ways to deal with this. Perhaps it would have been more helpful to let the bad moods just "be" and not get so personally upset by them.

Kurdt loved the neighborhood and all of our neighbors loved him. He was a real charmer when it came to the adults and children in our neighborhood. I had reports about how well-behaved he was, how good his manners were, and how nice he was to other children. I was very pleased with his social successes, but I knew we had to work on our relationship. Kurdt did not want anyone to tell him what to do. He had to learn that I was the boss in the family. This was a problem for him since, when he lived in El Salvador, he was used to being his own boss as well as the boss over his siblings.

Kurdt, whose face was usually brilliant with his beautiful smile or his mischievous eyes, could, on occasion, turn on one of the most repugnant sneers I have ever seen. One way to push my button is to sneer. On one occasion when I had set a limit for him, the content of which I no longer recall, his face turned white with anger and he turned on his vicious sneer. I saw red and lashed out at him and slapped his face. He became extremely upset and went to his room, where he stayed for a long time. I instantly felt terrible about the slap. I checked on him periodically but he refused to talk. I felt guilty and helpless at the same time. I never imagined I would slap anyone.

I went downstairs and sat in the kitchen and felt some tears roll down my cheeks. At that moment, Sara came up and said, "Momma, it's okay to cry." She'd heard me say those words so often and it was clear she had taken them in. I hugged her and thanked her, and I let myself know that Kurdt and I would work things out…maybe not today…but we would resolve problems as they came up. Perhaps these resolutions might take a long while, but we would work things out. He had twelve years to work out his ways of surviving and he would need time to incorporate new ways that fit his new life. He would learn to succeed with his intellect, charm and his willingness to persevere.

The major response Kurdt had to stress was withdrawal and blocking out anyone and everyone. Unfortunately for Kurdt and for me, this was one of the most difficult behaviors for me to deal with. I get upset when my existence is being blotted out. I do know, however, that withdrawal can save one's life. It's a positive when escaping a situation that threatens life, but a negative when attempting to resolve differences between people. What Kurdt needed to learn was that his life was not threatened at this time. He needed to learn how to identify and resolve problems face-to-face. This learning would take time, and we both needed to be patient to allow this growth to take place. We spent the summer getting to know each other, learning English, and getting used to totally different customs. I focused on having "fun" times. We had fun cooking together, cleaning, shopping, biking and many other activities. Memories of these good times would help us through the difficult times to come.

SCHOOL

When it was time for school, the kids were very excited. The school bus picked them up at the end of our long drive, where we had a shelter to avoid the wind. On the second day of school, Sara fell asleep on the school bus while on the way home. She missed her stop and the bus driver didn't even see her peacefully sleeping on the seat bench at the back of the bus. The driver drove into the bus lot and locked the bus. I was waiting for Sara to come home and when the bus passed, I got worried. I called the principal of the school and she was as worried as I was. Kurdt and I quickly hurried to the school, as did the teachers and principal. We waited for the bus driver, who was very surprised to see us all. She hurriedly unlocked her bus and a very sleepy child emerged.

"Oh Sara, what an adventure!" I called out, with a big smile on my face. I quickly framed the whole event as Sara's BIG adventure and gave her a story to tell. She had no time to get worried and loved all of the attention she got. More important…she didn't have time to feel afraid and experience the trauma she could have felt. She had enough old traumas to deal with; she didn't need any more. Instead, she said it was like being a princess with a lot of people clapping for her. I don't really think that she ever knew that this did not happen to every child that rode the bus. We also saw to it that this did not happen again. The bus driver agreed to be more careful.

School began in September, and Sara was put in the first grade since she needed a full day of exposure to the English language and she needed to be around the other children. The principal and I decided that she would probably spend two years in the first grade.

Kurdt was put in the third grade. He had to catch up in all subjects. Besides learning the language and learning how to read English, he had a long way to go to catch up in math and science. He was way behind his age group. We were fortunate that he had a wonderful male teacher, Mr. Philips. He really liked this teacher and it was a big help for him to have a teacher who also cared about him. He had a number of special education classes, but felt that people thought he was dumb, and he knew he was not dumb. School was very difficult for him. He started acting up and playing the class clown, getting his class to laugh. Kurdt's self-esteem was at an all-time low. He was definitely not the boss at school. I had thought that my childhood experiences with learning a second language would make me more sensitive to Kurdt's situation. When I thought about where I was as a child, there was really no resemblance to the children's lives. I had started school at age 2, could read…not English…knew math and science and I had always liked school. No one had beaten me if I got a question wrong.

When the children came home from school, I could tell that the world was upside down for Kurdt. He was sullen and angry. Doing homework seemed to be an exercise in futility. He started reading a first-grade book and I could see the disappointment in his eyes. There were many tearful moments mixed with moments filled with rage. I attempted to find books with story lines more in keeping with his age. I found some comic books that he enjoyed.

I spoke to the school about the possibility of bi-lingual classes, but not only did they not have the staff for this, but the language the children spoke was a brand of Spanish the teachers did not recognize. So we had to start at the very beginning. The kids would be in regular classes and take regular subjects. Everything would be taught in English. Sometimes, "new" is exciting. However, when everything is new and nothing is familiar, the world gets a bit scary. I was amazed that my early school experiences in this country were so similar to what Kurdt was living through. Although I felt his pain and frustration, I don't believe I was able to provide any more help than what my mother gave me. "I feel your pain" is not enough.

There were times when Kurdt would be angry and in tears. He would throw things about and kick what was in front of him. He was so frustrated. He would scream that he wanted to return to El Salvador. I could really understand him. I remembered how badly I had wanted to return to Belgium when I was a child. I tried to share this with him and let him know that things would get better. I told him that this time next year, he would speak English just like his friends. I don't think he heard me. He didn't understand me. I held him until he calmed down, but I don't believe I penetrated the "tough guy." I told him that he was an important part of our family and that even if he really wanted to return to El Salvador, that was no longer a possibility.

At this point I was already feeling like a failure as a parent. I had hoped that I could help the children make a smoother transition to their new lives than I had made when I was their age. I seemed to have failed in that. Kurdt seemed as miserable as I had been when I was faced with a totally different world and language. I had also lost the familiar support group I had relied on. I had also felt alone. However, I could not come up with a plan that would make this dramatic change in his life easier for him. While I was feeling miserable about my failures, it suddenly dawned on me that this "was not about me." I needed to focus on what would help the children. Perhaps I needed to accept the fact that this transition would not be an easy one, and support and guidance were the best I could do.

THE PHOTOGRAPH

The kids came with no personal possessions. When I picked them up in Cleveland, I got an envelope with paperwork and a five-by-seven photograph. I had put the photo away as there was so much to deal with, and came upon it several months later. It was a black-and-white picture of a relatively young woman who looked worn out, abused, and very angry. Her nose looked like it had been broken, and one side of her face was swollen. The most striking aspect of the photo for me was the look in her eyes. There was such a mixture of despair and rage that it was hard for me to continue looking. I pondered what to do with it. It was a terrible picture of a distraught person, but it was probably a picture of the kids' biological mother. Another instance of "what do I do with this?"

"Kurdt, who is this?"

He came running and as I handed him the photo, he just stared. After several minutes, he replied, his voice shaking: "That's my mother. She didn't always look like this. They probably told her to look angry when they were taking her picture. They always did that with people."

"Kurdt…who would tell her…"

But Kurdt handed me the picture and quickly ran to the other room. I was taken aback by his response to this photo. I wondered what this woman had been like to live with. I didn't know what to do with the picture. I thought the kids needed this picture as their mother had been important in their past and remembering was good

... usually good, anyway. I got a frame for the picture and put it on the mantle.

Several days later, I noticed the picture was missing. I asked Kurdt if he had borrowed it, and he said, "No, I didn't touch it. I don't want it."

"Sara, did you take it? It's okay if you did. It's a picture of your mom."

"I know, I know," she said, looking guilty as she continued playing with Snuggles, her stuffed toy.

What a mystery! Both kids looked extremely uneasy. I looked around some more, but didn't find it. Something was up about this photo.

Lorene, our housekeeper, found the picture in a pile of trash and gave it to me. "What a terrible picture of a very sad woman. Is it their mom?"

"Yes, and I agree that it is a sad picture." Without thinking any further, I put it back on the mantle. Within a week, it was gone again. The search was on again. And again, the photo was found in the trash. I should have concluded that someone did not want to look at this picture; it brought back too much pain. However, I made a duplicate and it went back on the mantle. The next time it was found, it was torn up.

I talked to Sara again and this time, in her broken English, she said, "I just didn't want to look at it...it was too scary...she was mean." She sobbed and sobbed. I held her and rocked her.

"You never have to look at the picture again. I should have guessed that the person who took the picture was upset about it. It would also have been okay for you to tell me how you felt when looking at this photo. You're not in trouble. I should have realized that you were too upset to have that likeness of your mom around. I'm sorry I didn't take it away sooner."

"It's okay, Mom, but she was a scary person. I don't want to think about her."

"What I will do is put this picture in my desk drawer. If you want to look at it, you can do so. It's important, though, that you do not tear it up. Some day, when you are grown and maybe even have children, you may want to see it again. It will be a time when it doesn't hurt so much to look." At this point, I dropped the issue. The remaining photo was put away. It is available for someone to look at it if they want to.

WORKING MOM (1981-85)

It soon became apparent to me that teaching family therapy and working with families in therapy was almost totally unrelated to being the Mom of two kids. There were some striking differences between the family stories I had read about in books and our family experience. I was definitely a neophyte in the realm of parenting. The books had made everything so simple. If you did this, then logically, this should happen. It doesn't work like that. My children had been essentially "street kids," and in El Salvador, they had very few rules to adhere to. They were used to doing what they wanted with no one to really guide them. Their basic goal each day was to stay alive. As I began to set some limits and give them some chores to do, battles followed when they realized the limits and chores were meant for them.

Parenting and child development books tended to focus on raising children from the moment of birth (or even pre-birth), not beginning when the children were ages five and eleven. Older children with a traumatic history are a different story. My reality of the long work hours and many parental duties struck home fairly soon. I was grateful that I was my own boss and that I could take the time I wanted for us to adjust to our new lives. I took some time off of work to get the rhythm of the children. I was able to afford a housekeeper, Lorene, for three days per week. She became a priceless family member. It was clear to me, however, that I was now a parent. I wanted my parenting style to be different from what I had experienced as a child. I wanted to be sensitive to my children's feelings, to be available, to know what questions to ask and when to ask them, and not burst into anger when I didn't know what to do. I wanted to be available when the kids had questions. I wanted to know what happened at school or at play. I really wanted to get to know my children. I wanted to smoothly move from home to work…no bumps. I was setting up a really tall order. I was trying to do something I had no model for.

Walking down the hill from the big house on my first day of work was difficult. I felt so conflicted. I wanted to work…BUT…I didn't want to go…I didn't want to leave the children…I was anxious. How would my clients deal with this major change in my life? I had been thinking about this and was aware that not everyone would feel ecstatic about my personal decision to adopt. I nervously opened the door to the office and saw that everyone in the group was present. That was good…I thought. People greeted me with a cheer, that was also good. We were off to an interesting beginning. Then silence.

One person finally broke the silence. "I want to work. I know everyone was cheering a moment ago, but I don't really feel that way. I'm not sure how I feel. I'm sad one moment and the next, I feel angry and then even glad. I feel a real mixture of stuff. I am happy for you and the kids and I know it is a good thing that you're helping them out…but I wonder what will change here. Will you be as available as you have been? And I'm angry that things are changing. I don't like change." At this point, he picked up a tennis racket and began to strike a pillow and yell.

"I hate you…I hate that you changed things and I didn't have a say. I don't like change. It's always bad."

As he sobbed, I stroked his back. Your feelings make sense to me. It's great that you are able to express yourself and feel what you feel and then share with us. This is a big change for all of you and I am aware of this. This is also a change that none of you asked for.

As the first client sat down, another spoke up: "I'm where he's at…I like what you have chosen to do, but I'm afraid. I'm fearful that you won't be there for me. You've always been available when I needed you, and now you have two needy kids."

"Believe it or not, it is possible to have children and work as a therapist. My schedule will be tighter with other obligations, but I will have time for you." As I said these words, I felt a sinking feeling in my stomach. Was this a promise I could keep? Am I telling the truth? Should I tell everyone that I wasn't sure how my schedule would work out and that I wouldn't be as available as before? As others spoke up and shared their worries, my anxiety grew. This was definitely uncharted territory for me. Everyone in the group shared and expressed a range of feelings from rage to sorrow as well as happiness for me and my family. I worked with everyone in much the same style as in the past. Motherhood had not dulled my brain. It was good work and I believe I validated people's feelings…BUT…I had to speak up with my truth.

"As you all worked and honestly expressed your feelings, I became aware that I needed to tell you what is happening in my heart. I will be there for you. At this moment, I need to honestly say that I will do my best to be there when you need me, but there might be times when my children must come first. Times when I need to change the time of an appointment or the length of an appointment. I'm just beginning the parental journey and I have to admit that I am a novice. I understand your fear of change and I can myself identify with this fear. However, I'm hoping that we can all take this opportunity to accept change and focus on the positive transformations we can initiate in our lives. It is important that we, you and I, remain truthful to what we are thinking and feeling and agree to share all thoughts, positive and negative, with the group. Agreed?" All spoke up affirmatively and nodded and the group was over for the night.

I did, however, have to decide that it was okay for me to do what was right for me and my children in spite of others having negative reactions. If people could not deal with the choices I made in my life, I would be willing to transfer their care to another therapist. My decisions were good for me and I could stop my second-guessing and anxiety about what others would think.

The one fact that everyone could agree on was that the change in MY life had a very real impact on those around me: clients, friends, and family. I had less social interaction with my childless friends and single friends than before the adoption. Interactions with others were different. What we spoke about in conversations was totally different. Is therapy easier on clients when a therapist's life is unknown? Probably yes. Is it better? I don't know. I do know that if my personal life were unknown to my clients, most would create a fantasy life for me that may or may not coincide with reality. This is transference, and is useful when it comes to analysis of life positions.

For the first month or so, while working with groups, it was much harder for me to concentrate on the people I was working with as I kept wondering what was going on at the house. Instead of directing my focal energy on my clients, my mind would wander to what were the kids doing, learning, experiencing? I thought… "What are the kids getting into? What are they watching on TV? I want to be with them; I can't…not now…I need to focus…pay attention to work…look at the people around me…the kids can get me later…these people need me now." Fear and anxiety possessed me as I wondered if I could be the therapist I had been. I used to be able to zone in on a myriad of minds going off in all directions around me. Now, my mind had never been so full of thoughts unrelated to the group I was leading. I needed to get a grip on myself. I used all of the energy I could muster to keep my focus on my clients.

I gazed out of the window, somewhat distracted, and what did I see? Superman was in my backyard.! There was my young son cavorting about the backyard, playing at being superman. He was wearing his blue underwear on top of his blue jeans and a blue towel served as his cape. He looked so happy, running as fast as he could…he was flying and whooping and hollering. Even watching him, I could get into the fun. My task, however, was to focus on work.

I hoped and prayed that focus on work would become easier as I adjusted to being a parent. I had thought about the impact of adopting children, but I had not really thought the situation through when it came to work. I had been prepared for my clients to have strong reactions to the adoptions, but I hadn't realized that I would have feelings I had never had before. Having children had changed the total focus of my life and I wanted that. With time, however, I hoped that separating from the kids at the house and moving cleanly into the therapy group experience would become easier. I had brought some unexpected conflict into my life and the lives of my clients. Hopefully, we would be able to utilize this experience in the therapy process. I also hoped that the newness of this dramatic situation would ease up and that I might glance at a child playing but not get caught up in the joy of the experience.

OUR FIRST YEAR AS A FAMILY

Our first Autumn was filled with new experiences. Falling leaves and huge piles of leaves perfect for diving into were exciting. The children hadn't really lived through the change of seasons we, in the northern climates, anticipate yearly. They marveled that their new world changed colors so dramatically. Leaves were green one moment and bright yellow or orange or even red the next. The ground even changed from green to brown. The temperature was suddenly much colder, not even warm temperatures in El Salvador. They suddenly had to wear coats to feel comfortable. They had never worn coats; in fact, they had never had coats. Something very new.

Sara loved her warm coat, and even appreciated wearing it. Kurdt, however, fought coats and anything that felt like an encumbrance. I would send him to school with a winter jacket, a hat, and gloves, and thirty minutes later, I would get a call from the school that Kurdt needed warm winter clothing. I agreed, and told them so. Kurdt did not agree, and had left his winter clothing in our bus stop. This went on for weeks, and I got tired of the phone calls and the recriminations. The school seemed to think that I had no idea that coats were a necessity in winter. I finally told the school that Kurdt had what he needed for a Michigan winter, and that so far, he was making decisions that did not include what we thought he needed to wear. I decided that since Kurdt was not getting sick, was not complaining, and was thrilled with the idea that he no longer needed to mess with his locker and the combination, that I was going to leave well enough alone and stop harassing him. The coat and all the winter gear were there if he wanted to wear it. The choice was his. The school was not happy, but they stopped insisting that their way was the only way. Toward the end of that first winter, Kurdt chose to dress for the climate. Winter was new to the kids and many adventures awaited them.

"Get up…get up," I said excitedly. It was late, and the children had been asleep for a while. "You have to see this."

Sleepily, Sara said: "Not now…I want to sleep."

"You will really want to see this. Put your coat on and we'll go outside for a minute."

Both kids said, "Okay," and we were off to explore the night time outside world.

"Oh…Oh…What is this white stuff?" exclaimed Sara as she stood on the patio which was covered with snow. She put her gloved hands out and squealed as the snow landed on her glove and disappeared as it melted.

"This is snow," said Kurdt as he gathered some up in his hands and made a snowball. He threw it at me and another at Sara. We all laughed and giggled our way to a hill where I had put a sled. Kurdt was the first to careen down the hill. He knew what to do with the sled and how to avoid the trees. Then he wanted Sara to go down the hill, however she was not as skilled as her older brother. He aimed her sled at a tree, and she bounced off the sled as she collided with the tree. Luckily, she was not hurt. I warned Kurdt to NOT aim for trees when it came to sledding. Both kids loved their magical night-time snow experience.

Another exciting moment during this first year was our first Christmas as a family. I had asked two of my friends if they could come to a Christmas party at the house as Mr. and Mrs. Klaus. The kids seemed to have no idea as to who Santa Klaus was, or even what Christmas was all about. I think they had never celebrated any major holiday. I don't even think that they went to church services. I know that they had never had any presents.

We had many friends attend our party, and after a while, everyone started exclaiming that Santa was there. The excitement was intense. Sara ran up to me, terrified of the strange man in the red suit. Santa was a strange, scary character for Sara.

"Who are you and why are you here? Why do people like you and why do you wear such silly clothes?" Sara asked, almost shouting her questions.

It took a while for her to calm down and then I had a chance to introduce her to Santa. It was a challenge explaining to this child who had very little experience with "magical" people…and to explain in English was doubly difficult.

On Christmas eve, we had a family celebration and opened presents. As I was growing up, we had always opened all of our presents in the evening. All was going well until we had finished and were cleaning up all of the paper and junk.

Sara piped up, "And now Santa is going to come and give me my real presents."

I was horrified. What should I say? I believed her. She really looked like she was expecting presents from Santa. Kurdt and I put our heads together and concluded that she really believed that the big time was after Santa came. We had no presents left to wrap up. All the stores were closed and everything had been opened. Sara was determined to go to bed and wait for what Santa would bring.

"Mom…what are we going to do? She's going to be so disappointed. I didn't know she believed in Santa," exclaimed Kurdt.

"We could look around and see if we find something that would do as a present. We could tell her the truth…there is no Santa. Wow…she will be so disappointed. I don't know how I missed the fact that she believed in Santa."

We looked around the house and found some nuts and candies and put them in her stocking. Before she went to bed, I tried to tell her the truth. I believe I tried, but didn't get very far. She believed in Santa Klaus and she was convinced that Santa would come with the big stuff. I guess I hadn't thought that she believed in Santa. When she woke up, she was devastated. She saw the nuts and candies, and knew exactly where they had come from. They were the Christmas nuts and candies from around the house.

So, this new mom had a lot to learn. I needed to know how to think the way a child would think. I was way too rational. I don't know how the truth would have fared that night, but it probably would have done better than continuing to try to cover up a mistake. I wondered for a long time where Sara got the idea that the really big presents are brought by Santa. At some point, I remembered reading **The Night Before Christmas** and other books to her. They all had plenty of pictures of Santa bringing huge packages. Sara is a really bright kid, and I'm sure she put the whole story together. Her disappointment in Christmas lasted. I think that, in some ways, Sara is still angry at me for not knowing that Santa brought the important stuff on Christmas Eve and the kids opened them the next morning. She was angry because she believed she was lied to, and I have to agree with that belief. I had never thought of all of the Christmas stories perpetuating lies, but in a sense, they do.

"Sara, in my home country of Belgium, we celebrated Sint Nicolaas day in early December. He was a real person who was very kind. We put our shoes out the night before his day, and we would get some little gifts the next day. We all knew the presents came from our parents, but we pretended that they came from Sint Nicolaas. Let's do this next year."

Sara scowled. "So are you saying that there is no Santa? That it was all a lie?"

"I wouldn't call it a lie…we were just pretending. No one meant for you to get hurt and we certainly did not want to lie to you. Will you forgive me for messing this up?"

"Okay…I guess," she said sadly.

For this first Christmas, my friends and I went overboard on presents. We had lots of decorations, lots of presents, and a huge tree. I did learn, but a bit too late, that giving too much leads to many problems. Sara later told me that if she didn't get what she wanted or if she got something she didn't like, all she needed to do was damage the present and she would usually get something she really liked. It was like magic. Not good! This was not what I wanted to teach my children. I had a lot to learn about manipulation. I'm sure that all of the new things coming their way felt like magical windfalls. They needed everything, as they only came with their shoes on their feet. They had been getting new things since they came in May. And Christmas brought more. No wonder Sara was confused about presents. No wonder she readily believed in a magical person who would bring all of these gifts.

During this first year, there were many very happy events at school. Sara was in her first play, and she had the role of a red bird. She danced around and didn't have to say a word. She looked wonderful in her red outfit. At home, she danced around the kitchen island and chirped like a bird. What fun she had.

Both kids enjoyed the various festivals and the food at school. Their favorite parade was Halloween. Sara was a bride in a white dress. Kurdt was a rock star. They loved going trick-or-treating with friends, and couldn't believe that people would give them candy. The Thanksgiving feast and parade were a lot of fun. Sara was her red bird and Kurdt was also in costume. They all paraded around the school and enjoyed an afternoon of play instead of work. For Sara, it seemed like school celebrated one party after another.

My friends and the school parents were very curious about the backgrounds of the children. I can't believe how many times I heard, "Oh, those poor children." I heard it so often that I began to worry that phrases like these would turn the kids into victims. I let people know that the children were survivors, not victims. I asked, "Please don't feel sorry for them." I knew that they needed to come to terms with the past, but I didn't want them to begin to use what happened to them as excuses for not functioning. I didn't want them to take on the mantle of "those poor children". It's too easy to envision yourself as a "poor thing" who has been victimized and then start feeling resentment toward others you start to blame. I was not raising two victims. They were survivors.

Other people would say things like, "How nice that they can start all over again." This is really an idiotic statement. The kids moved to a different country and to another family situation; they didn't have their past experiences excised from their brains. What happened…happened. People are sometimes so thoughtless. Past memories are always with you. Starting life all over with none of the traumas playing a part in one's life is not possible. The children had a devastating history that, at some point, they would need to deal with. My task was to accept this fact and help them sort through this process as best I could, not sweep issues under the rug. I don't believe in trying to get rid of the past, even the tragedies. Sometimes, facing the pain will make you stronger. The advice "don't think about it" just does not work.

I loved going to activities at school…the day trips to museums, factories, and historical sites. We would often go by bus, and I saw this as an opportunity to get to know some of the other parents. I was often approached by: "Are you the nanny?" I have to admit that I felt angry at this question. Just because I didn't look like my kids didn't mean I was an employee of their rightful parents. People do tend to be thoughtless. I decided, however, that I needed to move on from being angry and upset by this statement. I was the children's mother, and as long as the three of us knew this, that's all that mattered.

Neither child wanted to talk about El Salvador. They had learned enough English where I thought we could talk about the world they left behind, but NO…they had nothing to say. I was curious and had my suspicions as to their experience, but they got very quiet if I broached the subject. It's only as adults that they occasionally touch the subject of their past. They have both enjoyed being part of this memoir. During his first year in the United States, Kurdt was having difficulties with any form of direction. He did not like anyone telling him what to do. He was used to being his own boss. He had difficulties doing his schoolwork and homework, but did not like anyone to help him. I think he felt inadequate or put down when a tutor or I tried to help.

Toward the end of the first year, our social worker was preparing us to go to court to finalize the adoption. Kurdt had made his statement, "I want to go back to El Salvador," and she was shocked. She said that statement would really make a mess of the adoption and he had better say, "I want to be adopted." I wasn't sure what he would say, but I said a lot of prayers. I knew the judge would ask him what he wanted. He did, and Kurdt did say, "I want to be adopted by my Mom." I was thrilled. God had answered my prayers. I felt that my family was safe and grounded. We could work out our differences. You might wonder why Kurdt would want to return to the horrors of El Salvador. He told me at a later point in our lives that he was overwhelmed by the changes in his life…the new language, school, and the lack of control he felt over even simple things. He had been in charge of his world. He had been the boss. Professing in the courtroom that he wanted to be adopted was his declaration that he would work on dealing with this confusing world he had been "dropped into," even though he was mystified as to where this world would take him. He was experiencing a sliver of trust and was ready to move on. We were one step closer on our journey to family.

PROBLEMS AT SCHOOL

When Kurdt began school, he had to contend with a good deal of bullying. On one particular day, while in the playground, he had enough. He stood up to the bully and struck out and hit him. The whole school stood around and no one attempted to stop him. I think that most people thought the bully deserved what he was getting. When the bully fell down, Kurdt walked away, and the problems with teasing and bullying also went away. His fellow students cheered him on and a teacher helped him clean up. Nothing more was said about the fight.

School was not easy for Kurdt. He had many learning disabilities and I believe he was also handicapped by the many years he was behind in his education. He had to start all over with his classes. He understood nothing about history.

"Why would anyone spend their time going over what had happened hundreds of years ago? All of that stuff is over and done with…why talk about it."

I suggested that we could learn from history and perhaps not repeat old mistakes.

Kurdt yelled…"People don't learn…they are going to do the same thing over and over. That's what happens in El Salvador."

I had to admit that "there's a lot of truth in your belief, but hopefully, people can learn from their mistakes."

He answered: "Don't you wish."

We continued to have struggles when I helped him with his homework. I think he felt powerless, and keeping an image of power was very important to Kurdt. He needed to be in charge. Being in special education did not help his image, so he worked on being the class clown. He was very good at making people laugh. He also cultivated a gruff "I don't care, this is stupid" attitude which did not enamor him with teachers, but he was loved by his fellow students.

It was hard for Kurdt to put his energy into learning as there were so many distractions in his life. He tended to get into a fair amount of trouble. Nothing big like fighting, but annoying for me in that I had to appear at school each time. One of the incidents occurred when he was in the sixth grade. He was caught "rolling his baby down the hall." I was shocked…I had no idea what this meant. He apparently had to "look after an egg which represented a baby." Apparently, the purpose of this task was to make the student more responsible. Kurdt, however, wanted to "toughen his baby up by applying challenges like rolling it down the hall." I'm afraid that I thought the whole incident was funny and somewhat stupid, but Kurdt was an expert at testing limits…at home and at school. I did, however, believe that he needed to be willing to do tasks required of him even if he thought the work was dumb. As a child in El Salvador, if he thought a task had no merit or didn't make sense to him, he just did not do it and that was that. Nothing came of his refusal. In his new world, a boss at work could very easily insist that he do a particular task that he thought stupid, and it was either do the work or lose the job. He needed to learn how to work under people he did not always agree with. This was very hard for him.

When Kurdt began middle school, his clothing style changed dramatically. He chose black parachute pants and black tee shirts with heavy metal band logos on them. I should have said "no" more often than I did, as his clothing carried a message. At times, he even wore an earring with an upside-down cross. His clothing was meant to shock. It was, however, still within the rules of the school, so there were no complaints. He was a walking advertisement for oppositional behavior. I think I was waiting for the school to say "no," and when they did not, I let him keep this clothing style.

Kurdt's fellow students really liked him, but the teachers dreaded having him in their classes, in spite of also liking him a great deal. He was a distraction and created many opportunities for other students to laugh. Kurdt was very bright, but the schools failed to recognize this or capture his intellect. They succeeded in encouraging his oppositional spirit. They assumed that everyone learned the same way and they failed to identify Kurdt's learning style. There was so much to fight against. I had personally, always wanted to please and placate others, so I had trouble understanding the attraction of getting people angry or frustrated. Kurdt was the opposite. Kurdt's oppositional behavior was successful for him. People would get angry with him and...LEAVE HIM ALONE. I think he felt safer when left alone. Feeling safe was very important to both children.

One very significant incident remained a secret for several weeks, until a group of Kurdt's fellow students went to the principal and reported that a teacher had slammed Kurdt into a wall and banged his head. I had heard nothing about this until about a week later, when one of his friends told me.

"How could you not tell me about this? This is very serious." I screamed at the principal. He looked upset and seemed at a loss for words.

"Ah…ah…Let's calm down and talk."

"I want to talk to this teacher."

Reluctantly, the principal told me where to find the teacher, and I was surprised to learn that it was a teacher Kurdt really liked.

"Mr……We need to talk. I heard what happened in your class a few weeks ago. You slammed Kurdt into a wall and it sounded like you were in a rage."

"I'm so sorry that happened. Kurdt wasn't at fault for anything. My wife and I had twins the night before this incident and I hadn't slept. The whole class was acting up and Kurdt was the closest kid. I grabbed him and pushed him into the wall. I'm so sorry. That behavior was not excusable…I can't believe I actually did it… I've never lost it like that…I'm so sorry…What can I do?"

We talked for what seemed like hours and I understood what had happened. We talked about what his options had been. He was incredibly remorseful. He could just have called in sick. He agreed to attend some anger management classes, and I agreed to let this issue go. I insisted, however, that he apologize to Kurdt and make it clear to him that he had done nothing wrong. I told Kurdt what had happened during our talk, I also told him that if he was ready to let go of the incident that I was ready. He said, "absolutely," and he seemed happy that I had not made a "big stink" of the whole experience. Once more, however, I was not sure what I should have done. I hadn't realized the complexity of the problems facing parents on a daily basis.

Over the next few years, Sara progressed in school and worked on her schoolwork. She was very bright and was completely invested in school. One problem that she verbalized was that she had felt she had to deal with various looks of displeasure from teachers when they heard her last name and figured out that she was Kurdt's sister. They expected a disrupter and she had to work hard to change their opinions. In spite of awkward beginnings, her relationships with teachers were generally good.

One of the issues that Sara has talked about was that when she was in school, she lied a lot. She told stories that were ridiculous. They were stories that placed her in dire circumstances but she always ended up prevailing. One example was that she told a friend: "I almost died last night. I had a 105-degree fever and Mom took me to the hospital." Her friends were shocked and listened intently. It seemed like another way to get the attention she craved. No one told me about these stories and I wish someone had. As an adult, she still felt unhappy with remembering this failing and told me about it. In hindsight, I wish I had spent more time talking to her about her lying, as I did know it was an issue for her. She said she doesn't know why she made up these terrible stories. She has always felt ashamed of this part of her. She speculated that perhaps this might explain why she has been reluctant to stay in touch with school friends.

I was aware that Sara avoided acknowledging me while on school outings. I asked her what was going on.

"You're fat...we don't even look alike. I don't like having to explain who you are to me."

I felt myself tighten up as I pretended that what she said hadn't hurt me. "A lot of parents are overweight and don't particularly look like their children. I don't think I am any different from other parents."

Sara looked down and mumbled something I didn't hear.

With a little more time to think, I thought that she might have been looking for some ways that we were alike. It's a bit like "claiming" behavior… "She's got your eyes". She'd heard her friend's parents and family say, "Oh, you are just like your mother", and she wanted someone to say the same about her. At this point, I'm just guessing what her motivation might have been other than being hurtful to me. I knew that we needed to talk.

One way Sara might have experienced being different from her classmates was with respect to race. Sara and Kurdt were probably the only brown-skinned children in the school district. From what I observed, they were minimally teased, but any taunting is really too much. Kurdt reacted to racial slurs by fighting. Sara was treated like a beautiful doll, set apart from the other children. At the schools, none of the personnel and none of the parents talked openly about race. I heard some racial slurs, and was told, "When the kids get used to your kids, they'll stop. I wasn't happy with this response. Even though the slurs were not a continuous thing, I thought that any racial epithets were too much. I thought the school should look at this issue. My kids were the first Hispanics that I knew of in the district, but I could envision a much more diverse population in the coming years. There was no interest from the school when it came to taking this issue further and using this event as a teaching moment. I did not pursue the complaint. The kids were relieved as they were worried I would make a big stink and then things would be worse for them. Sara, in particular, had experienced no racial slurs and she was pleased with her friends and fearful of disrupting where things were for her.

Our first few years were filled with learning and more learning. On the whole, we got along fairly well. I grew to love both children with all of my heart. Kurdt, however, was growing increasingly testy. I think he felt the strain of everything he needed to learn. He was struggling against the demands school and home were placing on him. His rock band was consuming more of his time. As his English improved, so did his fund of foul words,

UMBRELLA GIRL

Sara has always been an incredibly generous child. She noticed the poor and the homeless and asked if there was anything she could do. I suggested and helped her bring food to the food banks and that she could help out in other places that needed help. We lived a distance from town so going to volunteer on a regular basis was difficult with my work schedule and the kids' school schedule. Occasionally, Sara went on outings with friends when I wasn't available.

I was a collector of umbrellas…beautiful, unusual, and relatively expensive umbrellas. I had a Winnie the Pooh and a number of umbrellas with animals or impressionist paintings on them. I have no idea why I collected these, except that they were useful and pretty. They were very colorful additions to wardrobes. Sara and I loved them. She would open the very fancy ones and twirl around and dance with them. When she was first adopted, Sara convinced me to purchase a little pink parasol for her. It became a fixture for her, rain or shine, until it disappeared. Kurdt, the tough guy, had no need for anything that would mark him as weak or silly and he thought that umbrellas, especially mine, would do just that.

Over a period of months, I started to notice that my collection was decreasing in size. I thought nothing of it, as I assumed that some had just not been put away where they belonged. I had been encouraging Sara to use them when it rained and so I thought they were just misplaced.

One day, while driving through Ann Arbor, I spotted an old man under a fancy Winnie the Pooh umbrella… "My Winnie the Pooh!"

Sara looked upset and exclaimed, "No…No…it's not the same. Yours is at the house. I'm sure of it."

I was suddenly feeling a bit suspicious. "Are you sure you don't know anything about THIS umbrella? Do you know anything about this gentleman…this homeless person who seems to be carrying MY umbrella?"

Sara's head went down and she began to sob. "He was so cold and it was raining and I felt so bad for him. I had to do something. I had an umbrella and I knew we had more at home, so I gave him the one I was carrying. I'm so sorry," she cried and cried.

I felt so sorry that I had made an issue of this gift.

"It was so kind of you to help him…you can tell me about this. You're not in any trouble. Did all of the umbrellas go to help people?" She nodded and I understood.

I thought about the many articles of clothing…gloves, hats and scarves that had also gone missing since the cold weather had set in. This was Sara's second winter ever. She had only recently experienced snow and bitter cold.

"Sara, do you know anything about the missing gloves and hats?"

Again, I saw tears and again, she nodded her head. "Yes, I thought they must be cold and we had lots. You would just get new ones when the others were gone."

I felt in a state of shock. I knew I had hit the motherload when it came to great kids. She was kind and very generous and genuinely wanted to share. I told her, "Yes, they were cold and it is kind of you to think of them. You are not in trouble for doing this; in fact, let's go and get more winter stuff and bring it to the shelter."

Sara smiled and eagerly nodded her head.

We made a habit of giving to those who needed help. I wondered how this child of seven managed to give things on her own. She was always with an adult. She said it was often when she was out with her school friends and it was raining or snowing. Her friend just thought that she had put things down and had forgotten them.

As I remember this episode in our lives together, I am still moved to tears. She had been a child who had nothing. She was blessed to be transferred to a world where she had everything, and from the goodness of her heart, she wanted to share.

BACK TO TRAVELING, THIS TIME WITH CHILDREN 1983-1987

I chose not to travel far from home when I first adopted the children. I thought it would be too traumatizing for them to leave a place they now knew as home. I waited a bit longer than two years. It felt like forever for me, as I really loved to travel and visit friends and exotic places all over the world. The kids were now fluent in English, but they were apprehensive when it came to travel. Once they came to the realization that they had a home, they were reluctant to take any chance of losing it. Much of my work involved traveling and working with people as trainees all over the world. I was ready to resume this, but how would things work with children?

We talked about the first place we would go, and the kids seemed fascinated with Australia, the land down under. They wanted to see kangaroos, emus, and koala bears. I told them it was a long, long way from home. They had no idea what I meant by long, but we created a plan. We would go to three cities: Sydney, Melbourne, and Adelaide. We would stay with families I knew at each stop. At this point, since language was not an issue, travel would be safer. It was summer, so the kids would not lose any school time and the trip would definitely be a learning experience and a lot of fun. We would spend one week in each of the first two cities and two weeks in Adelaide.

I had underestimated the trauma involved in packing our suitcases. I consistently told the kids that we would return home in one month. Everything in our home would be exactly as we left it.

The dogs would be well taken care of and they would remember us and they would welcome us affectionately. Their friends would all be waiting for them to return and would be eager to hear about their adventures. In spite of these reassurances, anxiety levels were high when it came to packing our bags. The kids were certain that they would forget items that were ABSOLUTELY NECESSARY and things we couldn't replace by buying them elsewhere. I had been packing my bags for years and never dreamed of the issues the kids raised. I gave myself a hard time for not planning some small local trips to get us all used to traveling and for the kids to experience coming home. "Oh well, opportunity lost." Sitting down, taking our time, and talking about our excitement and anxiety was definitely helpful.

Slowly, we got ourselves ready and we were off. I told the kids what to expect on the planes. "Planes…you mean we'll go on more than one plane? I don't know if I'm ready for that," exclaimed Kurdt. We sat down and went over our itinerary and counted the number of planes it would take to get us to Sydney. There were three planes.

We were finally ready to go to the airport. Our first exercise in patience took place at Detroit Metropolitan Airport. We had to go through the inspection line to get ready to go on the plane. Both kids had packed their own backpacks and…you guessed it…I forgot to go through them, assuming that it was just their stuff they were packing. When Sara's bag was being examined, a huge…very, very loud buzzer went off and police surrounded us. Sara let out a screech and an earsplitting wail and started to sob. One policeman took the bag and gingerly removed a very large pair of gardening shears. Things calmed down when they saw that a small girl had simply packed her toys and she needed scissors to cut her paper dolls. I was reprimanded for not checking the bag, and the scissors were thrown away. We were all a bit shaken up and when all of the officials went away, Sara was able to stop crying. I told her we had simply made a mistake, and that I should have checked the bag since I knew the rules.

I said, "Let's just chalk it up to beginning our adventures. This is the first story you can tell your friends about…excitement at the airport."

Our plane was slightly delayed, but I was assured we would still make our connection in Chicago. When we got to Chicago, I realized that if we got separated, the kids would need to know where we needed to be. We had talked about the trip but had said nothing about all of the airports and the various gates we needed to be at. I had mentioned our final destination to the kids but that was about it. I had a lot to learn about traveling with kids.

I asked Sara what she would do if we got separated. She knew our destination, and the airline we were traveling and had some idea as to the gate we needed to be at in Chicago. Okay…I thought. I was impressed. I asked Kurdt and he looked stunned and confused. "I don't know, maybe ask a policeman," he muttered. I quickly wrote our travel plans…planes, airports, destinations and pinned them to the kids' coats. Now, we were ready to go. We were going to have a wonderful time. The trip was very long and boring. Between movies, food, and sleep, we arrived in almost decent condition and were met by our friends in Sydney, Australia.

"Wow! We're on the other side of the world. Do you feel like you're standing on your head? I don't."

The kids looked confused, but when I showed them where we were in relation to where we live, they understood and also said, "Wow!" We were all excited to once more stand on real land after many, many hours of air flight. Our host family greeted us, and the kids were happy that we would stay with Australian kids. Both of the children we would live with were close to Kurdt's age, but Sara quickly made a place for herself. We settled into our home for the week, had a nap, and went sightseeing. We were amazed at the beautiful Opera House which was situated in the Sydney Harbor. The roof looks like huge sails, and the kids exclaimed that it looked like it would fly away. The harbor itself was gigantic, and there were a number of beaches. The beach we enjoyed the most was Bondi Beach. We saw a lot of people riding the waves on surfboards. Since animals were of great interest to all, our next stop was the Taronga Zoo. It was a very hilly, beautiful home for many animals. We were allowed to pet and hold Koalas and some incredible exotic birds. This was really exciting for the kids, but the kangaroos and their babies provided the thrill of the day…to see the heads of the Joeys peek out of their pouches was something we had not seen before.

In the evening, Kurdt and the older children partied and played a variety of games. Sara fell asleep, trying to keep up with the big kids. Our time in Australia was just beginning and so far, all was well. For the next three days I would be working. However, sightseeing trips were planned for the kids. The Australians had school, but the parents decided to give them a few days off so they could join in.

My workshops went well. I was able to focus and take my mind off the children and what they might be doing. In the evenings, Kurdt and Sara filled me in on what had gone on in the day for them.

They got to hike and spend more time in wildlife preserves, where they saw elephant seals, penguins, wallabies, and many animals they had never seen before. They really enjoyed their Australian friends. Sara reported that she really liked all of the playmates. The fact that she was considerably younger than the others was not getting in her way.

I was happy to see how well the kids were adapting to new surroundings and how easily they were relating to the other kids. Sara was a bit jet-lagged and crabby at times, but after a good sleep, she was her bubbly self again. Both kids were still a bit apprehensive about being so far away from home, but accepted reassurance that our house would be untouched until we returned. They were eager to learn about this new world they had only read about before.

Our next stop was Melbourne, Australia. It is the capital of the state of Victoria and felt like a big city to us. Since we came from a relatively small town, Ann Arbor, both Sydney and Melbourne were huge to the kids. There were art museums and again wonderful gardens. Once more, we stayed with a family with children and we were able to forge new friendships. I was again able to do my work while the children were with new friends. They discovered that many of the games they played were the same the world over.

I was thankful that everyone was getting along. The success of my work depended on the kids relating well with the people we were living with. Bringing two children on a work trip and having others look after them while I was busy was new to me, and I knew I was expecting a lot from our hosts. Even though this arrangement was part of our work contract, I had no idea whether or not this was workable. I knew that Kurdt could be difficult at times, and I hoped that he would not exercise any nasty behavior. A few days of disappointments or crankiness could make everything difficult. I worried about the kids and our hosts and functioning in my workshops. I was committed to a work schedule which included three work days per week. That left four days for the kids, but would that work for them?

I did not know how all of this would play out. The kids were in totally new surroundings, away from what had become their much-loved and familiar home, away from their much-loved dogs, away from familiar friends, and now they had to deal with a totally different brand of English, Australian English. At first they laughed as they were deciphering what was said to them. I was relieved when they enjoyed the differences in the languages and even worked on developing their own brand of Australian. They seem to be adapting to change very well thus far. When we left Melbourne, our first two weeks of vacation were over, and with the exception of a few minor conflicts, we were okay.

I had saved, for last, what I believed was the best part of the trip: a drive from Melbourne to Adelaide through the countryside and desert. As a grown-up, I should have been aware that a long car ride through what some people might call a "God-forsaken" area would not be the most exciting experience in a repertoire of possibilities, especially for children. I thoroughly enjoyed the beautiful desert areas with fauna and flora. This landscape is quite different from what we were familiar with in Michigan. Rather than enjoying this new experience, the children kept their eyes on their game boys and relished long snoozes. I had read in Wikipedia that Australia is the "oldest, flattest and driest inhabited continent, with the least fertile soil." I found this fascinating but the kids saw piles of sand. I saw all of the different colors of the landscape; the kids were bored. This long drive was definitely not exciting for children, so I hurried up and decided it was important to get to Adelaide quickly. We would stop if we needed to. I would certainly stop if the kids wanted to look at sites.

We got to Adelaide, my favorite place in Australia and had a great time. We stayed with Vanda and Bruce and their four children. The kids loved their time with this family as they went camping and horseback riding, two things that were new to them. They were able to walk among the animals at the Cleland Reserve and even got to hand-feed them. Kurdt was fun to watch as he hand-fed kangaroos. They got a bit closer than he felt comfortable. He had begun with one small animal and at one point, he had five large kangaroos, all wanting what he was handing out. It got a bit out of hand, so he threw the food some distance away and they all hopped over to battle it out. Kangaroos can be dangerous, so I had been getting worried, but he did the smart thing. Both kids enjoyed the exotic birds, all kinds of parrots, and big birds such as emus. We enjoyed exploring the outback with people who knew what was important and needed to be examined more closely. There were vistas where we could see for many miles and there was also a seashore and many wonderful beaches. Having never experienced sea and sand, Sara and Kurdt were excited running through the sand and the waves, whooping and yelling while splashing one another and their new friends.

The children were kept so busy that for about four days, I saw very little of them. In Adelaide, I worked for four days and saw them in the evenings. I missed them. Kurdt missed his buddies back home, the dogs, and the house. He had fun, but I could see that he was homesick.

More than sightseeing, we had the opportunity to explore some of the world together. I really enjoyed experiencing all of these new places, and some of my old haunts with the kids. I loved watching their reactions…their eyes in particular, and I was enthralled with the wonderful sounds of sheer joy when they saw animals and places they had only read about before. Seeing how people experienced life in other parts of the globe was a chance for them to grow. One such opportunity for Kurdt occurred when he was feeding kangaroos. It had been scary for him to be swarmed by five kangaroos but he solved the problem and he even owned up to being afraid. That was very new for him…to own up to fear. Learning takes place when one is open to participation in life.

My children were able to meet many of my friends, especially Robin and Val, and I felt I was able to introduce them to a very important part of my life. They didn't really understand what all of this was about…the traveling, the therapy groups, the marathon groups, or the lectures. We talked about my work and the kids asked my Australian friends, "What I did".

Their friends simply said, "She's a special teacher who helps our folks learn new things. Some people bring problems that she helps them solve."

I loved this first trip, even with its obstacles. I learned that for the kids, one of the complications of traveling was learning to say "goodbye." They had spent the last three years experiencing how to connect with people and how to trust. There is a lot of trust involved in verbalizing a simple "hello." For Kurdt, greeting someone is not a perfunctory behavior. It is actually the beginning of something meaningful. At the end of each stop on this trip, Kurdt had to find a way to disconnect from the people he had gotten close with. I discovered this was very hard for him. He did not like getting to know people, liking them, and leaving them. He was much more of a people person than he or I ever imagined himself to be. He decided he did not want to travel, at least not around the world. If he grew to love people, he wanted them nearby. It was too painful not to be able to reconnect when he wanted. Sara, however, continued to love to travel.

I made more trips back to Australia and Sara accompanied me on many of these ventures. Kurdt always chose to stay with friends at home. He stated that he really enjoyed our first trip away, but he felt grounded at our home. He said, "I have a home and I want to be sure it doesn't go away."

On one of our last trips to Australia, Sara, age eleven, decided to stay and do a term at school in Sydney. Since it was our summer, it was the winter term for the Aussie kids. The school welcomed her and gave her a schedule and she was off. She stayed with my good friend, Tricia and also with Acey and her children. She got a real taste of Australia. Tricia became "Aunt Tricia". Sara was impressed with the school system, especially the fact that uniforms were compulsory. She enjoyed herself, but was surprised that the kids didn't know where Canada was. She gave them pencils she had brought with her as goodbye gifts. They had Michigan embossed on them and her classmates loved them. She only had about twenty of them, so not everyone got one.

Sara reported that in Australia, she was the coldest she'd ever felt and didn't seem able to get warm. During our winters, we have central heating and fireplaces, so we are able to warm up completely when we come in from the cold. In Australia, they had fireplaces or wood-burning stoves, but no central heating. The front of your body could warm up in front of the fire, but the rest of you still was cold. Sara said she never felt warm through and through. I had to admit that I felt the same way when I visited one summer. She said it was interesting to experience seasons that are the opposite of ours. Winter was experienced in July. At the close of the school term, my girl came home, very happy to be back in familiar territory. Sara was somehow able to fly first class. How she managed to get first class is beyond me, but it was great. She said she had a good time and missed us.

Who is this?

Cousins

Australia

Robin

Robin, Sara, Me

Sara and Auntie Tricia
England St.James Park

Sara and Mom

Sara with OmJac 1984

6-1984 Sara with Marieka and her husband and Lisa

Sara learns how to ride a bike 1984 in Europe. Thanks to Marinus Huige

EUROPE AND FAMILY

One of the trips I took while the kids were ten and sixteen was a trip to Europe with the primary goal of spending time with family. A little bit of work was scattered throughout the trip. I had tickets for both kids, but Kurdt, at the last minute, did not want to go. Kurdt could probably have stayed with Derrick's family, but I didn't want to take advantage of them. I had a male friend from Texas who said he would love to stay at the house with Kurdt. Since I knew him and I had several friends who also knew him and vouched for him, I hired him. I did check his references, and since I was aware that he had had difficulties with alcohol in the past, I wanted reassurance that all was okay with him. While my friends reassured me, I still felt uneasy as I knew that looking after a teenage boy was not an easy task, especially for someone who had no contact with children. I hired him to stay at the house, look after the dogs, and keep an eye on Kurdt, in spite of my anxiety.

I thought that I could simply transfer Lisa, my niece's name, on the ticket I had for Kurdt. Not possible. I had to buy another ticket for Lisa. The trip was scheduled for one month. We were off.

Our trip was fantastic. We went to Belgium, the Netherlands, Germany, Austria, Switzerland and France. I was doing presentations at the International Transactional Analysis Association annual meeting in Switzerland and also presiding over Clinical and Teaching Member exams. I also had several workshops scheduled in other countries, but most of the time, I was free to explore with the girls. The trip became a wonderful bonding time for me, Lisa and Sara. I loved visiting with Om Jac, tante Molly, Om

Adri and many other members of my Dad's family, as well as my Mom's brothers and their families. Lisa was a young adult, and this was her first trip to Europe. She enjoyed exploring the countries we visited and even had fun trying out the tiny country lanes and getting ourselves lost. Lisa and I were trying to get to Bruges. We had a map but still ended up on a dead-end path and a cow pasture occupied by several animals. We laughed and laughed but ultimately got to our destination.

Both girls enjoyed getting to know some of their Dutch cousins, especially Marinus, who taught Sara how to ride a bike. Sara's first bike ride was a family experience with Om Jac's family. She managed to ride about 30 miles in this first ride. She never complained. We were all shocked at her endurance.

The three of us really enjoyed ventures into new places, especially Switzerland. The rides up the mountains were spectacular. There was so much to see and do. We all loved the mountains. The mystical aura of the mountains seemed to put me under a spell. I couldn't believe the beauty of the moment. The others felt similarly. We opened up to adventures and to each other. I got to know Lisa and really appreciated what a fine young woman she had become. My time with Sara also felt magical as I watched her experience the beauty of this world. However, I became aware that Sara was a bit jealous of Lisa and was competitive with her when it came to my attention. We talked about this and I told her that Lisa and I would do some grown-up activities but that I would spend special time with Sara doing some of what she wanted. I also told her that no one would ever take her place. I don't think she really took this in. I again said that Lisa would not and could not replace her. I told Sara that I wanted her as my daughter, no one else.

She smiled, and she heard me. We went on many outings with a focus on family, museums and shopping. However, the beauty of the natural world around us was much more significant in truly capturing our hearts, especially the many colorful flowers that dominated the landscape. There was so much to experience and we loved it all.

In Belgium, Lisa and I went sightseeing and ended up in Brugges. I love this very picturesque town, especially the large plazas and the many canals. The town has such an old-fashioned, almost medieval feeling about it. We decided we wanted to have a wonderful meal in one of the fancy restaurants on the plaza. We began with wine and decided to order chateaubriand with all of the trimmings. We waited and waited and waited and finally, the food appeared. We were famished, but the food did not look the way fine, expensive food should. It was overcooked and tough. The vegetables were soggy and overly soft. We had ordered rare meat and it was well-cooked. We did taste the food and…wow…what a disappointment. I know that based on what is polite in Europe…we should have said nothing. I was more of an American than I thought…so…we called the waiter over to our table.

"The food is not good…it is overcooked…tough…it is not rare". He argued we stood our ground. Finally, after saying we would not eat it a number of times…in a huff, the waiter took the food back to the kitchen. Again, we waited and waited and waited. About twenty-five minutes later, the waiter returned with our original plates, slammed them on the table and stated emphatically:

"Everyone in the kitchen tried this food and we decided it was good."

He left in a huff. Lisa and I were shocked and speechless. After a few moments, we looked at each other and burst into laughter. We decided to leave money for our wine and find another place. I know we did not display European manners, but we were true to our stomachs. It was a funny experience that we enjoy sharing to this day. It was clear, however, that returning food in Europe is not something that the average European does, no matter how bad the food was. Lisa and I learned a lesson in cultural differences. I have no idea as to what we would do in the future in Europe if we were served very bad food.

Everything had gone well on this trip, and we were ready to go home. We remained high from our experiences until we crossed the threshold of our house. As we opened the door, the dogs raced out in desperation. Kurdt was nowhere in sight. My Texan friend had fled the coop. It looked like the dogs had been held captive in the house for about one week. Piles of poop graced the floor. The smell was repulsive and repellant. No wonder the dogs had been so desperate.

The shock of what I was experiencing awakened me fully and suddenly, I felt terrified. What had happened to Kurdt? Was he okay? Was he hurt? What have I done leaving him? What a shock. We were all choking and on the verge of losing the little bit of food, we had in our stomachs. So this is why we were not picked up at the airport. Where is the Texan? What happened here? Suddenly, the dogs dashed back into the house, making sounds I have never heard come from dogs…yelps…screams…barks…growls…you name it. The chaos of the moment was striking. I could only stand and hopefully blot out this experience. When they settled down, the poor animals rubbed against my legs and cried.

Coming to my senses, I called Judy, Derrick's mom and asked if she knew where Kurdt was. It turns out that Kurdt had decided to live in his friend Derrick's barn. He was safe. He later said that he had not gotten along with the Texan, especially when the latter began to drink and act crazy. He was afraid to return to the house since the man terrified him, so he waited for us to return. In the meantime, he had felt safe with Derrick's family.

Guilt kicked in as I couldn't believe that my judgment had been so poor as to hire someone with a checkered past to be with Kurdt, who was only sixteen at the time. I had known that the Texan had had problems with alcohol but the people who had recommended him said that was a long time ago. I don't know what happened. It could be that the responsibility for a teenager was more than he could bear, and Kurdt was not an easy young person. Kurdt said that he began to drink and was too crazy to deal with after the drinking began. I was unable to contact the Texan and our mutual friends did not know where he was. I never heard from him or saw him again. I discovered that the bank account I had set up for expenses had been cleaned out. Luckily I had only put fifteen hundred dollars in the account. I filed no charges against him. I decided that he probably needed the money more than I did. I had no idea as to the kind of demons that may have plagued him. All I could do was get to work cleaning the house. I was grateful that Kurdt had the sense to look after himself and that he found a safe place for himself. I told Kurdt that I was proud that he took care of his needs. I was, however, shaken up by the situation and I criticized myself. I finally stopped beating myself and focused on the wonderful trip I had just experienced and I was not going to let issues like this take that superb experience away. Sara, Lisa and I needed to keep the positives of this trip.

In 1986, I planned another trip, this time to Singapore, Hong Kong, Malaysia and China. Sara was very eager to go with me, so I agreed to take her. I had one international meeting in Singapore, but the rest of the trip was to be a vacation. Many of my friends from the Western Institute would be on this trip, so I was eager to meet up with them again. This would also give Sara and me a chance to have some special time together. Kurdt stayed with Derrick and Judy, his mom, assured me that she would be there for him.

Sara was eleven years old and a strikingly beautiful child. She was still small for her age, had shining, black curly hair, large, expressive black eyes, and loved to wear colorful clothes. I mention this, because it never crossed my mind that traveling with a small, attractive female child could be a problem. I knew about sex trafficking, but had no personal experience with this. I couldn't conceive of the possibility that Sara could become a target of grown men who lusted after her. She was a child.

I had thought that during this trip, Sara would cooperate and settle down with friends when I was working, as my work time was limited. The friends were people she liked, such as Robin and Val, and they agreed to keep an eye on her while I worked. I should have had Sara also agree to this, as simply keeping an eye on her was not enough. Sara was being a child and playing cat and mouse with her caretakers. The Asian men who worked at our five-star hotel were attracted to her like bees buzzing around flowers. She was only eleven years old and was naturally flattered by all of this male attention. Some of these people were brazen enough to phone our room at night and ask to speak with Sara. I finally went to the hotel manager and complained about his staff. It seemed that I could no longer trust that Sara would be fine on trips to this part of the world.

She was not safe, and she simply did not believe me when I told her that the men who were following her around were not "nice people. It was almost like a game to her. She loved to flirt and loved the attention she got, but she was just a beautiful preadolescent. It was as though she felt immune to danger. She thrived on attention and this was more than she had ever experienced. It was like a fairy tale come true and she was the princess. I reiterate…she was a child. I thought a part of her was seeking a father. Unfortunately, in the far east, many men are ready to be sexual with a female child.

In Singapore, when I complained to the hotel management that his employees were being inappropriate with a child, I did not get the response I was looking for. He treated this behavior as though it was an everyday occurrence. And maybe it was. It was almost as though the manager was saying, "So what?" After my complaint, the swarms seemed less intense, but I observed they were still there. We were able to do some sightseeing.

We loved how clean the whole city was and marveled at the fact that spitting out gum or throwing trash indiscriminately could get you a jail sentence. It was a beautiful, people-filled, colorful city and we did enjoy our time, in spite of the fact that I felt like a bodyguard. It's a shame that the idea of "cleanliness" didn't extend to the morality of the city, as the sexual attitudes toward children certainly brought a stench to this "clean city" for me. I was relieved to leave Singapore and Sara and I were off to Hong Kong. Maybe we would find a world that was safer for children.

We got to Hong Kong and enjoyed Chinese New Year on a ship in Hong Kong Harbor. Male interest in my beautiful child continued and I maintained my position of bodyguard. Sara continued to be oblivious to the danger around her and played her game of hide and seek. She eluded me at every turn. The fireworks were amazing, but even in this glorious setting, I had difficulty keeping Sara in my sights. She kept trying to escape from my custody and I felt like a warden with a recalcitrant prisoner.

It was like a cat-and-mouse game with Sara, as I needed to keep her near me and she did everything she could to escape my control. She kept wanting to slip away and do more exciting things than celebrate with her mother. She had no sense of the dangers this part of the world presented for her. She had no idea that many girls were kidnapped and sold as sex slaves. The target group for these kidnappings are children her age who just happen to be beautiful. Sara just thought what was happening was a fun game. She had no idea that her life was at stake. I felt the danger all around her but she remained oblivious to it. She just smiled and laughed and loved it when she got the men around her interested in her.

I hoped we could continue the trip to China and Indonesia, but I ended up canceling the rest of the trip for us after spending some time in China, only to have this craziness continue. This involved disappointing many of my friends who were also on the trip. I feared for my daughter's safety, which I saw as much more important than anything else on the agenda. Sara and I returned home early and I decided that staying home with the kids was where I had to be for the time being. Home was where we needed to be. Putting the kids at risk made no sense. Sara was just too young to understand the repercussions of her behavior. A part of her was still too innocent to believe that people could do horrible things to her and that she could be the victim. Perhaps it is still way too early for her to learn what some people do to innocents. I would stop my international travel

for the time being; I needed to spend more time as a stay-at-home
Mom.

SAFE TRAVEL AND FUN

Being a single parent limited my options, and I accepted that. I certainly did not feel good about the decision to limit international travel for the time being. I loved traveling and the work I did with so many people. I knew I had to make a choice and that, at this moment, the kids' needs came first. It felt as though I was shutting down a significant, creative part of myself. I would find other outlets for this part of me. I did give myself permission to take trips within the United States as long as I took a responsible person with us to stay with the kids when I needed to work. I was very lucky that Derrick's mom, Judy, was more than willing to take on this role. More importantly, I personally knew her to be a responsible adult. The kids looked up to and obeyed her, and I really enjoyed her company. We were able to take a wonderful trip to Aspen, Colorado and take Derrick and his mom with us. Judy agreed to keep an eye on the kids while I did some workshops and worked on exams.

We started early in the morning; in fact, it was still dark. An hour into our trip, I heard a very loud "thump" and discovered that I had managed to hit a deer. The sleepers in the van woke up with a start as we wobbled across the road and finally came to a stop at the roadside. The deer was a dead mess and I called the state police.

"I just hit a deer on Highway 696."

"Do you need help?"

"No, the van still runs and no one is hurt but the deer."

"Feel free to take the carcass with you." said the very pleasant policeperson.

"No thanks. Can I just leave it?" I asked.

"Of course, have a good trip." Miss 911 declared cheerfully.

The car still worked, but we needed to get it to a dealer. We were going to take the ferry across Lake Michigan and the car would have to make it until we got to a dealer in Wisconsin. The car survived the ferry ride across the lake and we made it to the dealership.

"It'll take two or three days to repair. Will you folks be okay while you're here? Asked the very friendly shop manager at the dealership.

"Yeah…we have a nice motel and if we can get some of our stuff, we will be fine," I said, feeling exhausted.

We decided to enjoy ourselves. The food was good at the motel and everyone enjoyed the pool. We did have a near mishap at the pool as it was overcrowded and Sara almost drowned. She was rescued by a man near her. Although we were all at the poolside, none of us noticed that she was in distress. We were all grateful for her rescue and that we were still in one piece. We were free to continue our trip after two days in the shop. With some difficulty, we survived thus far.

We had a great condo in Colorado and we were able to do some exciting things. The boys rafted the Colorado River and we still have wonderful picture memories of this experience. There were so many great activities and we did not have a single dull moment. Well…maybe toward the end of the trip, there was an occasional "I'm bored." It was an absolutely beautiful setting. Sara enjoyed her time with Judy and the other children at the conference. Kurdt and Derrick were always off to something. The air was crisp and clean and the breezes seemed to kiss our faces. Walking and hiking were more than exercise. They were mystical experiences. The food and the shopping were great. Sara and I enjoyed the wonderful boutiques and the beautiful clothes we were able to purchase. I was able to join in many of the fun times. We even got to meet John Denver at a party and that really tickled us.

John Denver sang for us and most of us were thrilled. He saw Sara and asked her, "What do you think?"

Sara answered, "Eh…" and shrugged her shoulders.

Everyone laughed, even John Denver.

I felt as though I had finally found a pace that made sense. My work had gone well and I had fun with the kids and my friends. I had found a way to marry travel, family, work and fun.

STORMY WEATHER

Dark clouds on the horizon were forecasting coming storms. I feared the battles I was experiencing in my home. The kids and I had been getting along fairly well for about five years, but I knew that we were moving into stormy territory. Kurdt looked for every possible opportunity to fight with me. He wanted control over his life and he was furious with me and with himself that the world was not going his way. He was not doing well academically and while he pretended this did not matter, I knew that it did and so did he. The only thing he felt good about was his heavy metal band, but he felt disapproval from others about this activity. His language became so foul that I can't and won't even put it on paper here. He made threats that he would injure Sara and me, and we were frightened of him. It is significant to note that no matter how enraged he became, he never lifted a hand to harm anyone. He did, however, put his hand through the wall on several occasions. He was in turmoil and refused help. He did not want to talk about any issues. He locked himself up, and would not look inside of himself for answers. He would throw things and swear, and in many ways, he was demanding his freedom. It became harder and harder to live with his rage permeating every square inch of our home.

I was afraid that Kurdt would get out of hand. To protect Sara, I asked my Mom to come and take her to St. Catherines and let her spend the summer in a safe place. She'd dealt with enough of Kurdt's rage. I knew that if I confronted Kurdt, I didn't want Sara to have to experience what might come of this. I was now in a position to deal with my son and Sara had a wonderful time with Aunt Ria and Grandma.

I did not want to involve the Juvenile Court as I had worked for another court system before and had some idea as to how they would deal with our issues. They would probably conduct interviews which, where Kurdt was concerned, would only increase the intensity of his rage and I could envision him acting out, forcing the court to ultimately put him in the juvenile home where I believe he would not learn anything positive. I did not want him to have a record that would follow him throughout his life. Kurdt was fighting with me and I was the one who needed to respond. I couldn't hand him over to a government agency and let them do battle for me. I concluded that this was a crucial turning point in my son's life. His rage and confusion were coming to a peak, and he needed space and help when it came to working out what was troubling him.

Part of Kurdt's problem was me. He had never quite gotten used to a woman being in charge of anything…especially not him. The model of the woman he was used to was subservient. I was unlike any woman he had ever met. He had put up with me for four years now. I was unlike any of his friends' mothers.

None of his friends had big homes, or had mothers who had traveled the globe lecturing. Why couldn't I be more like them? I had positions of power, but what did that say to Kurdt? At first his rages were occasional, but as time went on, this negative behavior was almost continual. He screamed that he wanted to be totally in charge of his life. He didn't want curfews, responsibilities, school, church, or anyone telling him what to do. The more he screamed, the more I knew that he wanted to run away from the closeness that was growing in our family. Lack of physical and emotional closeness had brought him pain in the past and now he wanted none of it.

Before he was adopted, violence dominated his life experience. He was beaten, shot, and had seen his biological mother killed…but he had been the boss….he had been in charge…he took care of his sisters. His best moments as a young boy had been when he was alone, free from adults, playing on the garbage pile next to the shack that had been his home. Grownups brought him grief. On his own, he had nothing…but the pain was not present.

At this time, I didn't know much of Kurdt's history…much of it he told me so that we could write this book. I needed to help him deal with this storm of feelings in a safe way. I had him see several male psychotherapists but this was not helpful. He attended an Outward Bound experience run by therapists and although he enjoyed the trip, he had gained nothing that would help him when it came to his feelings and behavior at home. Our medical doctor checked him out for drugs and all of the test results showed he was using nothing. I was pleased and surprised about this. I needed to take stock of his strengths, and this was one…no drugs. Another strength was his choice of friends…he chose smart, responsible people from good, intact families. His friendships were strong. Once he said "hello," he would not say "goodbye."

I knew that I needed to take some action in response to this crazy behavior. I was aware that as relationships become more intimate, panic may set in, especially with someone who has experienced traumatic events in childhood. I believe that Kurdt was beginning to love and respect me, and with this love came his fear of losing me. I remembered that Kurdt didn't want to do long distance traveling because he didn't want to say goodbye. Much of my thinking at this stage involved guessing, and to some extent, relying on past experience. Perhaps Kurdt believed that the closer one gets to a loved one, the greater the chance to get hurt…to be abandoned. Providing some distance often alleviates panic and rage and provides opportunities to do psychological work on these issues. Distance, while living together in a single residence, even a big house, is not easy to come by. Providing emotional and physical space gives a young mind an opportunity to think and problem-solve instead of automatically moving into a flight response. Taking care of himself in this world would also be an eye-opener for him and he could experience that it is not easy to be on your own in the United States. In spite of the difficulties involved in caring for oneself, both parent and teen benefit from the increased distance, as long as frequent contact in a safe place is maintained. Even minimal contact would be more than what we were experiencing at this time.

I did a lot of guessing at this point. I surmised that Kurdt and some of his friends were planning something. I think he was planning a major clash with me…a fight that would justify his leaving home. I assumed that he was planning on breaking free from the house. I thought that he would make a big scene of some sort so that "running away" would be a logical outcome. I think that part of this scene he envisioned would have me crying, losing control and doing everything in my power to keep him home. These were guesses on my part.

If he tried something like the above, I knew that I would not be able to stop him from leaving even if I wanted to and I wasn't even sure that I wanted to stop him. In fact, I was pretty sure that trying to stop him from leaving would be a terrible idea. I believed then as I do now that emotional space is a great healer and gives time for growth, IF POSITIVE CONTACT IS MAINTAINED DURING SEPARATION. Luckily, I liked Kurdt's friends, and felt that they would not be toxic and lead him further astray. However, no matter how I looked at it, I would be taking a big chance that space, time, and safe contact would give him what he needed to mature. I also knew that letting Kurdt move into the world by himself would give him an education in what it takes to survive in the real world. I was actually gambling that the relationship we had already established would be strong enough to see us through this battle.

I knew that permitting Kurdt to leave the house could put me in difficulty with the juvenile court; however, I knew that we desperately needed distance. I did not want to report his behavior to the court as I didn't want him to have a record and I thought they would probably make things worse. I didn't want to lose my boy. I was certain that we could resolve our differences. If we were going to be able to work on a meaningful relationship, we needed space, and more space than our home provided. I had friends in other countries who allowed their teens to move into an apartment near the family home, at the expense of the teen, while they focused on the relationship. These situations had worked out well. The children learned that life outside the home on your own is not easy. They learned a lot about responsibility. They were also kept busy with part-time jobs so that they could afford their freedom. They learned that freedom does not come cheap and requires a good deal of work. They also learned that expressing rage toward anyone who provided a different view of the world was an indulgence they could not afford while on their own. In other words, freedom has its limits, even when you are your own boss. I hoped that Kurdt would absorb this wisdom when he was "free". As I read this paragraph to myself, I can still hear myself trying to talk myself into taking the steps I knew I needed to take.

I loved Kurdt, but I knew that closeness was a major issue when it came to our relationship. He clamored for independence, but I now believe he was really terrified of loving and needing people…especially me. His nasty behavior produced distance…and ultimately, safety. If I allowed him to move out, he would not have to fight for his freedom to choose a safe distance; he could come and go based on how HE felt. I never dreamed that I would be thinking these thoughts. I felt pain when I thought about what I knew I needed to do. I did not want to do it. I knew, however, that I wanted him in my life forever, just not in the pathological way we were relating. He is my son. I knew that with some distance, he could work out his fear of closeness and perhaps find some respect for powerful women. My goal was to ultimately have a good working and loving relationship with him. I loved Kurdt! My commitment to him was forever, and I was willing to do what I believed would help us build on our love. I also knew that Kurdt loved me. I was prepared to take a big chance. Many paths would be available to him. He could allow rage to dominate his life direction. He could choose to terminate the relationship with the family we had worked so hard to build. He could continue with his job and school and spend time with Sara and me and good friends. I knew I needed to make a great deal of time to talk with him in neutral zones. I prayed that he would take this opportunity to learn.

It was critical that I devise a plan, and I had to act before Kurdt did. Significant in the plan was having his clothes packed as well as other things he might need. Everything had to be in the entryway, visible on first entering. It was all-important that the doors be locked so that he would need to ring the doorbell. I had to prepare myself. It was vital that I be in control of my feelings as the plan depended on me speaking clearly and calmly. I needed to stay near the front door. I had to maintain control over the feelings and what came out of my mouth. I knew I felt anger as well as sadness. But it was fundamental that I let my love for him dominate the tone and tenor of my words.

Kurdt rang the doorbell and I answered and welcomed him inside. He had come home from school with his friends. As I opened the door, I was faced with three glowering boys ready to do battle. However, as Kurdt crossed the threshold, he looked shocked. He saw the luggage. I was prepared. I told him that I would speak first and then he could speak. I said:

"When people behave as you have been behaving, it is generally a sign that they want to establish their own homes. They want to be their own boss and they don't want someone else telling them what to do. I accept that. You do not need to fight me for your freedom. You are now your own boss. I emancipate you. Emancipating you does not mean that I do not love you. I love you and you remain a very important part of our family. As family members, Sara and I would want us to have frequent lunches and dinners together. We can spend time talking and sharing where we are with each other. You and I need to work on our relationship by spending time together in neutral zones. You will need to eat anyway, so we will find restaurants we like."

I kept my voice low and spoke slowly. I didn't give him a chance to speak until I was finished. I worked hard to keep the tears from my voice and eyes and partially succeeded.

Kurdt's eyes were enormous. His face, which had initially been graced by a very angry, surly expression, went from ashen to perplexed. He had been prepared to storm out, and now he was quiet and didn't quite know what to do. He looked nervously around the entryway and his eyes shifted from the suitcases in the corner to me. He was silent. He stood frozen in place; his friends were equally still. Kurdt understood what had happened on a visceral level. His anger was gone as he and his friends picked the suitcases up and put them in the car. Kurdt stood by the car, pausing as he contemplated leaving.

As he left, I said, "We won't always have this anger separating us. I know this is probably hard to believe now, but we can work this out. I am still here for you. You are still my son. Call me when you have an address and a phone, and we can get together. I still love you."

Kurdt was shocked. He looked gray and his head was down. I felt a deep sadness as I watched him get in the car. I couldn't believe this was happening. I struggled to stay positive and forced myself to continue to see this as a good thing. I needed to believe that we could resolve this problem. I dissolved in tears as I closed the door.

Kurdt moved in with a friend and the friend's dad, and for the next eighteen months, he consistently went to school and worked hard at his job. I gave him no money, but brought him food frequently. I kept in close contact, letting him do his laundry at home and going out often for various meals. I paid for the restaurants. It was hard for me to admit that I had moved my son out of my house. I had many sleepless nights. Sara and I spoke with him in person and on the phone frequently. Restaurants became safe places where we kept our manners and were able to converse with a normal tone of voice. We all felt safer. Distance worked for us. It was important for us to accept that both sides needed to work on how we related. I think that the three of us knew we would work out our differences. None of us was interested in giving up on what we had. We knew we could plow through this "block". We took time to really get to know each other. We actually saw much more of one another than before our separation. I had a much better sense of what was going on in Kurdt's life and I believe he also knew me better. The rage that had permeated our interactions in the past slowly dissipated. We were able to laugh and enjoy one another's company. I saw him growing up to be a gentle, fun-loving young man. I recommended him for a job with a builder and he seemed to enjoy this job.

After about eighteen months, I approached Kurdt: "We've been getting along very well for the last year. What do you think?"

"Yeah…I've enjoyed my time with both of you. We do get along now."

"What would you think about moving back in with us?"

"Boy…I have to think about that. I have one request…I don't want a curfew. How would that go with you?"

"That would be fine with me. You've done very well setting your own curfew so you would be free to come and go as you please. Just let me know your schedule."

"Great…I'll move in tonight. Will that work for you?"

"I'd love it."

My beautiful boy was back. We took on an incredible challenge and succeeded.

HOUSES AND MOVES

Moving Kurdt out of the house was traumatic for both Sara and myself. Kurdt's destructive behavior had required strong confrontation. Once he was on his own, I spoke with him frequently and so did Sara. Actually, Sara started carrying notes for Kelly, Kurdt's girlfriend, and Kurdt. She rode the school bus with Kelly, and they often sat together. Kurdt's frightening rage dissipated, and we again had wonderful times together. Separation worked as we all felt safer. No one needed nastiness. Being aware that we were all personally in charge of how close or how distant we wanted to be gave us all permission to enjoy one another. We felt safe as we all knew we could leave when things got uncomfortable.

1986 through 1988 were difficult years for me. I cut down on my work so that I could be more available to the children, and I was finding that keeping a large house, an office, and thirteen acres of property was becoming a bit overwhelming. As a mother of two, life was increasingly complex. Each day, I was faced with choices that related to what I could now afford, what I now had the time to initiate and complete, and what I now had the personal energy for. I wanted my time and energy to go to my children. I also wanted to earn enough money to keep us comfortable and to pay for college. Years ago I had thought raising two children would not really change the routines in my life, particularly since my practice was out of my home. Not so…As a single mom, I felt a bit like a contortionist. I had a good deal on my plate. I limited my practice somewhat, especially since problems with Kurdt, and I was becoming increasingly aware of costs. In the past, if I wanted something expensive, I just worked a few more hours or set up a therapy marathon weekend. My hours had been my own. Not now. I decided I wanted a smaller place, less property, less work, closer to schools, with easy availability of groceries. I sold the property.

Kurdt was still living with his friend and attending school in Ann Arbor. Sara and I had felt lost in our large home. I had previously thought a great deal about selling the property and buying a home or building a place in the Ann Arbor School District. For some reason I thought the kids would do much better in a district that was more diverse. Kurdt had not done well in Dexter, as he had a multitude of learning disabilities that the schools had not addressed, but Sara was doing exceptionally well. How do I choose? I thought that Sara would do well in either of the districts and that Kurdt was more suited for Ann Arbor. When Kurdt would be ready to return home, we would need to live in Ann Arbor for him to continue in the school he was attending. I chose to purchase some property in the Ann Arbor school district, and I decided to build a home.

I sold my home on Valentine Road, and all three of us were incredibly sad. We loved that house and the neighborhood, in spite of the work living there entailed. The new build would be within biking distance of their old friends' homes. I hoped that Sara could maintain some of her friendships in the neighborhood. Moving out was a painful experience. I discovered that I was more attached to the place than I thought. Also, I had so many possessions, books, furniture, and many odds and ends. We had an auction, and everything was gone within four hours. Sara and I rented a house in Dexter and she got to walk to school for the first time. The school was right next door to us. I rented an office from a pediatrician friend, so I did have a place to work. This was a different way of life. Simpler in some ways, since the new house would be paid for, but there is a lot that can be said for working at home.

Both kids were very cooperative, but very sad. Kurdt was still living with his friend, but he was very involved in the sale of the house and the building of the new place. We still miss that property. If Kurdt could afford it, he would buy the Valentine Road property. I can understand all of my reasons or rationalizations for selling; however, I wonder if it was the best move for the kids. Sara had the hardest time with this move as she missed her friends and school. I had failed to take into account that as a new middle schooler, she didn't drive, and maintaining friendships would be much harder. Relationships are so intense in middle school; many friendships have long been established, and for Sara to have to start over with a new peer group really complicated her life. The move did not bring an improvement in Sara's life. I don't believe that I will ever know if this was the wisest thing to do for all of us. It's the best I could think of at the time.

It's interesting that one of my complaints from my childhood was that my parents never discussed the moves we made with my sisters and me. Change just happened and we had no input. As an adult, I realized that I left my children in the dark when it came to major decisions, and that it complicated their lives, as it did mine. I think that I actually defined talking about problems as "whining" and so I avoided sharing any issues as they arose. I didn't want the kids to feel burdened with my worries. When it came to taking action, I didn't even try to cut back on costs or try other measures. I didn't have a family conference where we could talk about all of the issues we were confronting. I certainly did not learn from my childhood experience. It was like I was on automatic pilot. My impulsive thought was that a move would resolve all issues. I was wrong.

Although life was feeling a bit chaotic, I decided to build a new home and chose a recommended builder. There is nothing like adding chaos to chaos, and I seem quite good at that. It does make life exciting. I did look at homes that were already built, but they did not have the space that would be large enough, private enough, and sound proof enough for my work. I wanted to build a specific area in the house for therapy. I knew it would not be as private as the separate twelve hundred square foot building on the old property, but it would be more private than anything I saw in available houses. It took eleven months to build the house I had designed, and there were problems galore. I found out way too late that the builder's credit was very bad. This meant that in order to get needed building supplies I would have to pay at the time of delivery. This included EVERYTHING for the house. (shingles, wood, concrete, cabinets, etc.) I was grateful that I had money in the bank.

"Jim (the builder), am I to understand that I have to be here and sign for everything that comes to the site? Do you understand that this level of micromanaging will be problematic for me?"

"Sorry, I'll see what I can work out."

So, I became the general manager of the project,…very time-consuming. I did, however, enjoy the building process. I learned a lot about building a house, and a lot about what makes me tick. I even pounded in a few nails. I also chose everything for the house, including a fancy and expensive front door. The builder's lack of credit affected the number of crew on the site, how quickly other tradesmen were willing to do work for us, and a wide variety of issues that required cooperation from others. We limped through the construction to what I was hoping would be the finish.

When we began the process of building, Sara and I moved to a house in Dexter which we left after five weeks of battling armies of insects. We did not dare bring any kind of food into the house for fear of it being devoured by the very hungry bugs in possession of the home. We ate out or had picnics. Sara enjoyed walking to school and she was now close enough to school to attend the after-school events. I got a taste of town life and decided it was great to be close to everything…stores, restaurants, etc. The last time I was able to walk to all of the necessary stores in town was when I was a small girl in Lokeren, Belgium.

When there was a large opossum killed by a car outside our front door, Sara insisted we put it in a plastic bag and take it to school for extra credit in science. It was fun to see how horrified and yet excited the teacher was. She very quickly called the Department of Natural Resources. Sara got her extra credit. In spite of the bugs, we enjoyed ourselves. After a few months battling the bugs, and after school closed for the summer, we moved again.

We rented a home in Ann Arbor for the summer, but our place was not finished by the time the owner returned. We ended up living in a small trailer on our property. I do have to admit, however, that Sara and I spent a good deal laughing throughout this unpleasant experience. The last week we spent in the trailer, Kurdt joined us as he decided to once more live at home. He was working for the builder. Living in the trailer simplified his life. I forgot to mention that we also had two dogs living with us, Lucky and Van Halen, throughout this test of our ability to live happily together. I can't believe how much fun we had during this ordeal. After Kurdt moved in, we often had fart wars at night. We were doubled over with laughter.

We lasted about a month or so in the trailer, and then moved into the unfinished house. I needed to put some pressure on the builder to get him to finish the house. I could think of nothing other than all three of us (five, including the dogs) moving into the house to put pressure on the builder. We had no occupancy permit and moved into the basement. The stairs to the main level of the house were not complete. The heating system was not available, but we bundled up and camped. We could not cook any food or even boil water. In fact, there was no water yet. The builder picked up some speed and we finally…after about a month…had a finished home.

It was a beautiful, contemporary home with many windows. The house was in the middle of four acres and we enjoyed planting some trees, especially three large evergreens, to represent our family. My friend Tricia came to visit from Australia, and she was convinced that the home was possessed by an Indian chief. She insisted she saw him. We had had significant problems with black flies in the house, and Tricia said it was because the chief was unhappy with our decision to build on his land. Sara agreed with Auntie Tricia as she said she also saw the chief. I did not. Those flies were definitely a problem, though…and we didn't seem to be able to rid the house of the infestation. After two years, I sold the house, and I still managed to make money on the sale. I now wanted to live in the heart of Ann Arbor, walking distance to stores and public transportation. Again, I made decisions without much input from the kids. Hindsight is amazing! Isn't it?

I bought a new duplex in Ann Arbor. I thought we could live on one side and I could use the other side for work. Both sides had three bedrooms and two full and one-half baths. It would even be perfect for out-of-town visitors and marathons. I loved the place and so did the kids. The grocery store was right across the street and all of the bus routes were available at the two stops right out our door. This was exactly what I was looking for. This was not to be, however, as I soon noticed problems with the house. We had the home inspected on purchase, however, the inspector missed some important problems. I first noticed that the trim around the doors had loosened and the doorways were sloping. I checked other areas and saw cracks in the foundation and cracks in some walls. We had a problem. I had another inspector check the house, and he concluded that the duplex had been built over a creek. Wow. The problem could be fixed, but it would take time and there would be no guarantees that the house would be fine. I made the builder buy the property back, pay for our moving expenses, and give us time to find a new place. I would be made whole financially, but I would not have this perfect place for my work and family. I have to admit I was sad. I found a place that was in the process of being built across the street from the duplex. We could stay where we were until the house was finished.

Another move. At this point, I was definitely feeling the need to settle down in one place. We had done enough moving. Sara was ready to find a place to settle in and stay awhile. Kurdt was very occupied with Kelly, and thinking of major changes in his life. He was thinking of graduating from High School, attending community college, and marriage and starting his own family. Sara was struggling with school and relationships. She had not adjusted well to leaving her Dexter friends and was struggling with making friends in a new school and a new town. Everything was different and adapting was not easy, but I felt like we could meet all the issues that confronted us at this time.

Kurdt on roof of our new house

Kurdt the builder

Our house

Kurdt and Kelly wedding

Kurdt + kelly   Sara + Gerrv

The Huiges

Kurdt and Reece

Kurdt and Kelly's twins: Audra and Dominic

Sara's children: Anthony, Matthew, Natalie

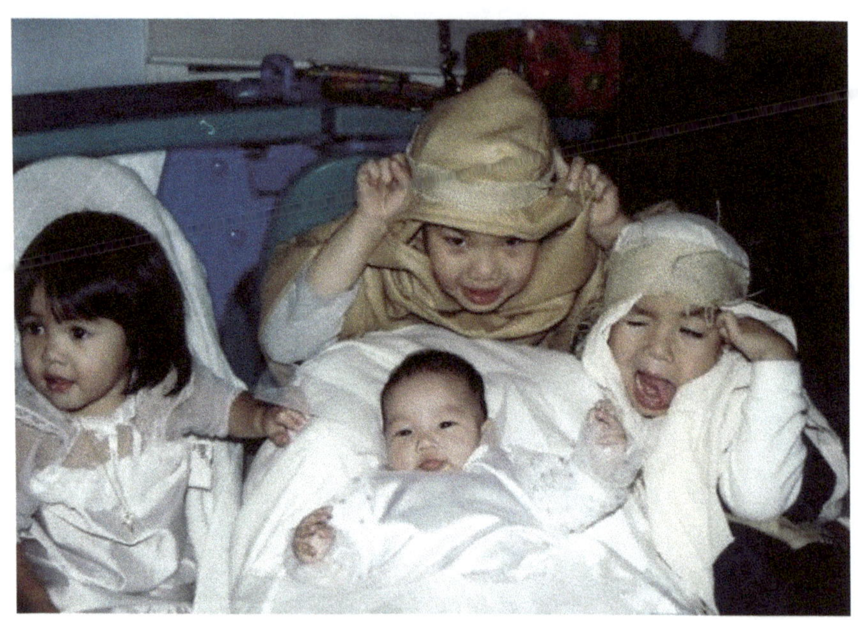

Grown up Now

APRIL 3, 1990 A DEATH IN THE FAMILY

I will never forget this day, April 2, 1990. I felt like a mess from the moment I woke up. Nothing was going right. I was fighting with everyone and I knew that the problem was me. Nothing felt right with the world. I was angry with the kids, but I knew they had done nothing wrong.

I felt so strange. I wanted to run away. I didn't want to be where I was. I wanted to be anywhere but where I was. I got in the car and started driving. Where was I even going? I went on auto-pilot and suddenly found myself headed towards St. Catherines and Mom. This was a four-and-a-half-hour trip. Something was wrong and I needed Mom. Something was wrong and I didn't even know what was wrong. Mom would help me. I had never felt this way before. I was afraid.

I drove like a person possessed. I was so rattled at Customs that the agent asked if I was okay. I told him, "Yes, but I got some bad news." I lied, but I had to make something up, and it felt like I was getting bad news from somewhere in the universe. I was assuming that something bad had happened or was going to happen. The road was long and boring. I saw one farm after another: hay stacks, cows and horses. Would I ever get there? It seemed like forever.

I had to get to Mom. By the time I reached London, I needed gas. I got out of the car and the fresh air revived me. I walked around and bought a snack. As I breathed in the air, I told myself that I was being foolish. It's true that I was very upset, but it still made no sense to me. I needed to get a grip on myself. I needed to go home and be there for the kids. It was 1990 and life was busy. There was no time to be taking crazy trips to Canada. I could see Mom when my schedule permitted.

I went home and felt like a fruitcake for this very strange behavior. The kids looked at me with worried expressions on their faces. Sara was busy studying and preparing for her confirmation. When I told her I almost went to visit Grandma, she said she wanted to go and share her confirmation journey with her. "I really love Grandma and I want to tell her about everything I'm doing. She will love hearing about it. She said she would come to my confirmation and I can't wait."

I felt myself settle down. The strange feelings of impending doom subsided somewhat, and I thought that given more time, I would feel whole again. I wasn't there yet. It was like some terrible premonition had made a home in my brain and I had convinced myself that something terrible was about to happen. I had to repeatedly shake myself and convince myself that all was once again right with the world. I continued to tremble for the rest of the day. I had a fitful night, waking up frequently with nightmares.

It was around noon, and our phone was ringing. I heard it, but I did not want to answer the phone.

Sara yelled, "Mom…the phone!"

"Got it…Hi…" I heard sobbing and suddenly realized that Ria was on the phone.

Anxiously, I needed to know what was happening. "Ria…calm down…what's going on? Speak slowly because it's hard to understand what you're saying."

"Mom is dead…she's dead…I couldn't do anything to help her. She just dropped dead. I don't know what I'll do without her." Ria's sobs were deep and sounded so painful. It was hard for her to continue.

"What happened? How did she die? Was she sick? When did she die?"

"We had been shopping and then stopped for lunch…" gasping for breath… "When we left the restaurant and Mom was about to get in the car, she just collapsed and died. I tried to revive her and the ambulance crew that came also tried. I knew she had a DO NOT RESUSCITATE ORDER but I'm glad everyone ignored it. I can't believe she's dead." Ria continued crying and turned the phone over to Lisa.

"Auntie Kris, can you come quickly? We need you."

"We can leave in about an hour. See you then." I said tearfully

I was in shock. I regretted not having completed my journey to Canada yesterday. I could have spoken to her one more time. I might have been there with her when she died. I couldn't believe she was dead…gone…forever. It's as though some part of her had called to me, but I told myself I was just being silly. I'd gone back home to look after the kids, but they were really old enough to look after themselves for a few days. I just hadn't listened to Mom's call. I didn't recognize it. Mom had tried to reach me to tell me there was something wrong with her. I knew there was something amiss in the universe, but didn't trust my instincts. All of yesterday's upset made sense to me now. Mom was dead! I can't believe she is dead. Not Mom…she was supposed to live forever.

The kids and I drove up immediately to be with the family. We were silent most of the five hours it took to get there. No one had anything to say. Sara cried a good deal of the way. Kurdt looked stone-faced, but I knew he was also in pain. He also loved Grandma deeply. We didn't even play music. Sara was heartbroken that her wonderful Grandma had died and would not be there to help her celebrate her confirmation. Grandma was very spiritual and Sara felt that she really understood what this ritual was all about and they had been looking forward to sharing this event.

I wanted, but did not want, to see Mom. I still couldn't believe she was dead. Seeing her or touching her would be proof that she was no longer alive, and I didn't want to validate her death. We visited Mom at the funeral home, and I could not look at her at first. She was so quiet and she did not look like Mom. The funeral director had put make-up on her face but she had seldom used it, so she looked different. Her face had never been the color of the makeup they chose for her. What I had the hardest time accepting was how quiet she was and she totally lacked energy. She was so "still." She was not present. I wanted her to sit up and join us at the party. She was so cold. The expression on her face was not the same as the Mom I loved. I'd never seen her so still and so quiet. This wasn't real. This wasn't real.

I spoke to her in my mind. "Mom, how dare you go! I want you to come back. I'm angry with you for dying. I'm not ready. I still need you and the kids need you…but …I know this is where you want to be. You're with God now…Oh, how I miss you!"

I felt so sad…I can't ever remember feeling so sad and empty. This is what I had been afraid of for a good deal of my life. I was so afraid of life without Mom…I felt I could never survive. I have never felt so sad and so empty. As I write this down, I remember how I felt. I was truly alone now. I had always feared losing Mom and now it had happened.

Everyone in the family was in shock. Ria and Lisa were grieving for the duration of the time we were there. Everyone loved Mom so much.

I was shocked that at the funeral, the church was completely full. Mom was an old woman of eighty-two, and yet she had many, many friends. Everyone had a story to tell about how she had touched their lives. There was also laughter at the funeral, as many of the stories were funny and said a lot about Mom's sense of humor.

One of the wonderful experiences during this time of grief was when my sisters, my children, and I went through Mom's things. I was surprised that she had so little when it came to material things. She had no money, as she had been living on her social security. There were a few pieces of jewelry, but nothing worth very much in terms of money. As we went through her clothing and some books and cards, we laughed and told our stories about Mom. Her favorite item of clothing had been a housedress which she wore anytime she wanted to be comfortable. It still had her scent. We cut it up and we all got a piece. We sat on her bed, holding our piece of the dress, and talked and talked. I don't think I had ever felt so close to my sisters. The most surprising request came from Kurdt, who wanted his grandma's slippers. Sara wanted grandma's shoes. We laughed and told her they were big shoes to fill. She said, "I know and I can do it."

I have always been overly attached to Mom. I was afraid of people and the world, and I felt somewhat safer in Mom's presence. It didn't really matter to me that Mom was as afraid of the world as

I was. Reality was not part of this relationship. It was hard for me to talk with her and I think equally hard for her to share thoughts and feelings with me. When I moved to Ann Arbor, I chose not to see her for more than a year. This was difficult for both of us, as Mom thought I was angry with her. The truth was that I was afraid I would lose myself...my very being...if I continued to live with her and even spend time with her. I needed to spread my wings and fly on my own, and Mom did not understand that. I needed to separate from her. I know I hurt her during this time. I don't believe she ever understood. She was my hero.

A GROWING FAMILY: KURDT'S IN LOVE 1994

The kids were growing up. I can't believe how fast these years have gone. Of course, I did adopt them as older children, so time at home was somewhat curtailed, but they are becoming adults and I already miss them. The hurried days of adolescence are almost over. The high energy in the house is dissipating and I'm beginning to hear the quiet again. I don't know if I'm ready for that.

When Kurdt returned from his time living with his friend, he was a changed man. He was now a man! He was easy to live with, cooperative and caring…and love was in the air. He was dating his childhood sweetheart.

Kurdt and Kelly were friends from the moment Kurdt first rode the school bus in the United States. They spoke and laughed and got to know each other and learned to appreciate each other over the years. They were the same age, but Kelly was several grades ahead of Kurdt. This made no difference in their friendship. When he was sixteen, Kurdt transferred to the Ann Arbor schools and at that time, it was Sara who helped to maintain this relationship. She shuttled messages back and forth between them. She was still riding the bus with Kelly, and became something of a go-between. Somehow, the young couple continued to see each other through Kelly's university years and Kurdt's high school and community college times. I supported their relationship as I also began to love Kelly and thought this could be a wonderful match.

Kelly's mom and dad were not initially thrilled with the idea that their daughter was involved with a "troublemaker". Kurdt had a reputation for trouble at school when he was at Dexter, and he was even blamed for getting Kelly kicked off the bus. It was apparently true that neither of them had done anything wrong that time, but they were both blamed for this particular incident and kicked off the bus. Kelly's mom was mortified.

"How could you think of dating that troublemaker?"

Her daughter had never been in any trouble. This was true. Kelly was one of the truly "good" kids in school. I have to admit that this was one of the many reasons I loved that Kurdt chose to date Kelly. She was beautiful and her spirit was even more spectacular.

Kurdt was confused and angered by Kelly's parents' response to him. "I don't understand why they don't accept me. They act like they don't like me."

I told him, "If Kelly were my daughter, I would respond pretty much the same fashion as her mom and dad. From what they know about you, they can't conclude that you are a prize package, and that is what parents want for their daughters. You look tough and talk tough and they have yet to experience the responsible part of you. They want someone who will work as a team-mate with their daughter and be a good dad to any kids that come along."

\ Once Kurdt quieted down, I told him, "You need to work hard and generally woo them. You need to show them kindness and thoughtfulness. You need to work to get them to open up to you." Whether it made sense to him or not, he worked at this relationship. He mowed their lawn, did work around their home, joined their church, and when Kelly's dad needed caretaking, he was even there for that. He won them over.

So, Kurdt married his grade school sweetheart. Kelly graduated from college as an occupational therapist and Kurdt got his associate's degree as a computer-assisted designer. Several years into their marriage, they had their first child, Alex, a beautiful, curly-haired boy. Around the same time, the company Kurdt worked for moved out of the area, and Kurdt was without a job. Both Kurdt and Kelly were reluctant to have their baby in childcare. They didn't want strangers raising their child, so they decided that Kurdt would stay home and look after the baby. Kelly's job had a good salary and benefits and she became the primary breadwinner for the time being. Kurdt became the stay-at-home daddy, and he was definitely a good one. I'm sure it took a lot for him to put all of his macho pride aside in order to take on this role.

Kurdt and Kelly were definitely tested with the birth of Alex. When he was about eighteen months old, it became clear that he had major problems. He became extremely angry when entering or leaving situations, was fearful of inanimate objects such as fans or vacuum cleaners, and seemed to have limited abilities to calm himself. It was difficult to bring him anywhere. His speech was considerably delayed. He had many deficits in communicating his needs and did not seem to understand emotions. I suggested to Kurdt that Alex was on the autism spectrum, but he became very upset and rejected my diagnosis. He was furious that I would suggest that his child was not perfect…that he had a flaw.

Later Alex was diagnosed with Autism by the family doctor and Kurdt and Kelly began to work with him. They educated themselves with respect to this diagnosis and after much trial and error, they had considerable success with their much-loved son. At school, Alex had a helper and a special education program to help him. School was a struggle and the Huige's met their challenge. They were often at odds with the school system when it came to deciding what was best for Alex. Kurdt had to fight so that Alex would have the regular High School Diploma. The school wanted to give him a certificate. It's as though they had written him off as hopeless from the beginning, and it took Kelly and Kurdt to fight for him. Dealing with the school system was continuously difficult. Alex is now a loving and hard-working young man of twenty-eight. He is able to live independently and is a great employee. He is quite good at making friends and enjoys life. At this time, he is sharing an apartment with his brother, Dominic and goes to church with his maternal grandma.

When Alex was about eight years old, his family was expanded by two when the twins, Dominic and Audra were born. The work really doubled for Kurdt and Kelly. They still had a great deal of work with an autistic child and now had two more babies. Too much to do and too much to think about. It was wonderful that Kelly's mom, dad, brother, sister and their spouses and families were all ready to help and provide support. I did what I could, but between work and Sara and the distance between Kurdt's family and my home, I had a limited amount of time available. Alex loved being the big brother and tried his best to be helpful; however, he did not quite understand that mom and dad's attention now was shared with the babies. In spite of having to share, he loved playing with the little ones and couldn't quite understand that they weren't old enough to play the way he liked.

Kurdt and Kelly had their hands full. Things got a bit easier when the twins were old enough for daycare and then school. When they got to middle school, Kurdt again got a job in his chosen field. However, when the twins were ten years old, a new little bundle of joy, Reece, was born. Once more, Kurdt became the caretaker of the home, and he did a great job.

For both Kurdt and Kelly, involvement in church has been foremost in their lives. Kelly has always followed the Methodist faith, and Kurdt chose to follow suit. I was grateful that he chose to be involved with church and God and I believed that a family needed to worship together. The denomination they chose was up to them; I was grateful that religion was important in his life. I am a Catholic, but according to Kurdt, his religion believed that Catholics are evil and would not be saved on the final day. At some point, Kurdt reassured me that this dictum did not apply to me. I was grateful that I was at least out of the evil category. My reprieve did not extend to spending alone time with children, as he was still worried that I would be a bad influence on them because of my religion. I was sad about this, but I was thankful that family and church family provided support Kurdt's family needed it.

Kurdt is a staunch conservative. This is the kid who wore black clothes with "Black Sabbath," and sometimes he even wore earrings that were upside down crosses. When Kurdt was young, getting him to church was a definite challenge. After his marriage, he and his family often go to church several times a week. Kurdt and his kids have been involved in wonderful social justice projects. I love that the Huige's are very involved with church. Even now, we occasionally have arguments about religion. At this point, we have chosen not to talk about religion and politics.

Kurdt's whole family is very involved with the outdoors and sports. Kurdt and the kids enjoy bicycle rides, running, camping and road trips around Michigan. Several times during the summer Kurdt will bring the kids over to our pool for swimming fun.

STRUGGLES WITH SARA

Sara spent the early 1990's struggling with high school. She had not adapted well to the change in school systems. I wish I had been more thoughtful when it came to school. I didn't need to settle for the public schools; there were other options. She had the bad luck to finally win a place in a school she enjoyed, Community High School, only to have it close down for renovation the next year. She chose a Catholic High School for grades ten and eleven, and Huron High School for grade twelve.

I thought that the larger school system would be more accepting of racial differences and would be more open-minded. I was really wrong. Sara was bullied and made fun of with phrases such as "I chink I see you…chink, chink, chink." This teasing began on day one and continued through high school.

During her teen years, we had more than our share of battles. It felt like we argued about everything. It seemed to me that the tougher school life was, the more we argued at home. From my perspective, she chose to do everything she wanted. In many ways, she was a very typical teen and she did what many teens do: rebel and argue. The last thing she wanted was to talk to me, listen to me, or follow any advice. As for me, I think I was spending too much time "telling her what to do" and not enough time listening to her. I found one of my diary entries that stated: "She is at the age where she knows everything and listening to others is not on her agenda." It sounds a bit like we were not listening to one another. I am regretful.

I made the mistake of buying a small car. I was busy with work, and driving her wherever she wanted to go would have been a real problem for me. I ignored the fact that we lived in an area with very good public transportation. I had not insisted that Sara do any work or even pay anything for the car. I, myself, was not clear on who the owner of the car was. Had I been clear on these issues, I would only have had to say, "Give me the keys…the car is off limits for a week, and if your attitude continues, the time will be extended." There were no ground rules around the use of the car. Since I had laid none of this groundwork, she just proclaimed, "The car is mine, how dare you take my keys." I don't know why I was so much more lenient on Sara than Kurdt. Somehow or other, I felt that Kurdt was on solid footing. When he was at his nastiest, we had the "car talk," and he did not change his attitude. I responded firmly and quickly. I ended up selling the car he was driving. He was angry, but he dealt with it. I trusted that he would not hurt himself. I was not convinced that Sara would look after herself when confronted strongly. Kurdt's acting out had been of a more different, direct nature…kind of "in your face". I was worried that if Sara got angry, she would act out sexually. In a lot of ways, I felt ill-equipped to confront her. I was worried that if she took off in an angry huff, she might get into serious trouble. She might have a serious accident, get pregnant, or get into drugs. I wasn't as sure of her friends as I was Kurdts". There had been a time when I was fearful of his anger, but somehow, I trusted that he wouldn't go crazy if I imposed limits. I was not even worried when I had him move out of the house. I knew that somehow, he had the inner strength to pull his life together. I wasn't so sure of Sara.

Speaking of all this recently, Sara asked me, "Mom, why didn't you impose limits on me like you did Kurdt? I needed that…didn't you see what I wanted from you?"

"I'm sorry…I wanted to clamp down on you, but I was afraid of what you might do…I was afraid that you would hurt yourself. You seemed so alone most of the time when there was no boy in your life, and when you did have a boy in your life, I worried that you might get pregnant. We did have one royal battle which really frightened me. Remember. You had a boyfriend who lived in Flint, Michigan…about one and a half hour drive from Ann Arbor. You went up there frequently. One snowy evening, around 10 p.m., you insisted that you wanted to go up to see him. I said you could not go…it was too late for a teenager to drive all that way alone.

"Oh yes, I am going," you screamed.

I was grateful that Kurdt was home, as I didn't want to deal with you alone. I tried to take your keys, but no luck. You dashed outside and into the car and locked the door.

"Oh no, you're not," I said…and I spread-eagled myself over the hood of the car. I was in my pajamas and slippers, and my only hope was that I would keep her from moving the car. Basically, I was gambling that she cared enough about me not to go…and that she still had some of her senses about her.

"Sara, for God's sake…please come to your senses and get out of this car. I'm not moving!" I yelled.

"I'm going…I don't care if you freeze to death…you'll give up and I'll go."

I was freezing, but there was no way I was going to let you win this battle. The snow was coming down thicker and faster. "Come on, God…give me a break…let up on the snow." The more snow that came down, the more determined I was. We yelled at each other and Kurdt begged for us both to go inside. After about an hour of this craziness, you capitulated and went into the house. I got the keys. I was wet and frozen and looked like a mess, but for some reason I began to laugh. You took a look at me and also began to giggle. We were a mess, but we were both thankful that this episode was over. For some reason, laughing felt good. Kurdt joined in and we went into the house and treated ourselves to hot chocolate. I really needed it. The whole episode, however, really shook me up. I felt successful when it came to setting a boundary, but I wasn't so sure that I could do it again. I can't believe the amount of energy this took.

The spring following this event, Sara's boyfriend graduated from high school and they decided to move into an apartment. I did not want this but I did not fight it. Sara was working and going to school, and these were behaviors I supported. I also wanted to remain on her "good side". We had spent time together since the major uproar described earlier, and I worked on solidifying our relationship. I think I was afraid that she would discard me. Just as with Kurdt, some distance did make it easier to get close and deal with uncomfortable issues. One such issue arose when Sara got kicked out of Catholic school because she was living with a boy. This was not a surprising event, as she had gone against school rules. She now began her final year of high school at another school, Huron High School. There was so much conflict in her life, and it was taking a toll. She was upset a good deal of the time, but she did manage to graduate.

After several months of living together, Sara left the apartment, since she had been doing most of the work. Not only was she working a job and going to school, she was supporting the two of them financially and paying all the bills. She was doing the clean up, laundry, and other things. The good-looking young man just sat around watching television, and his unwillingness to pitch in got old very quickly.

Sara asked to move back in with me and I agreed. We talked about how living together could move more smoothly and agreed to work on our relationship. We talked and talked and laughed. We seemed to grow more accepting of one another. I sensed that there was a lot that we were not sharing, but we were doing much better than before, so I felt happy with our progress.

PREMONITIONS AND PAIN 1995

With the kids almost grown up and independent, I thought the time was right for me to once more agree to do some workshops abroad. It had been a while, and my friends had been asking if I was going to resume traveling. I was surprised to discover that I did not miss either the excitement or the stress of going abroad…in fact…I loved being home with the kids. The excitement they brought into my life had been amazingly refreshing and wonderful. I loved being a Mom. I felt as though my intense concentration on parenting, reminiscent of our early years, was no longer needed. Everything I had to accomplish seemed so much easier. It was hard for me to fully understand the degree to which my life had changed. I had opened up so many parts of my heart and felt enriched beyond belief. These were MY children and I felt blessed.

It was 1995 and I was scheduled to take another trip to Belgium and France. I thought I would start out with a short trip of two weeks. I chose a short trip not because of kids at home, but because I just didn't want to be gone for a long time. I might miss something important and I know I'd miss the kids. Kurdt was no longer living at home, as he was married and living in Coldwater. Sara, however, was home again, and we were enjoying each other's company. She made it clear that I was not to worry about her. She would be fine.

I began packing for my trip, and rather than feeling elated about seeing old friends and traveling once more, I felt a pervasive feeling of impending doom. I felt it throughout my body. The visceral feeling was overwhelming. This was unusual for me. I always had a little bit of anxiety about flying, but this felt over the top. It was as though some disaster was about to happen. I was unhappy about everything. Nothing felt right with the world. It felt like I was having a premonition that something very bad was about to happen. I had had a very similar feeling the day before Mom died. Something terrible was wrong with my world...I argued with Kurdt when he called me...I fought with Sara...I argued with others and I really wished that my Mom was still alive. What was going on? I have to stop myself. Why am I making all of this stuff up? My inner voice screamed at me to stay home. I decided I just could not give in to this hysterical part of me that suddenly stuck its head up. If I gave in to this, I'd find myself homebound, and I did not want that. (1995)

I packed reluctantly and left, deciding that I would be careful. I had made a commitment to do three workshops and I had never failed to show up. This was my chance to again build up my international practice. This was the first time that I did not want to take an overseas trip.

The plane trip was uneventful and I thought I was over the anxiety hump. I began the workshop in Louvain and all seemed fine. It was wonderful seeing my friends and catching up with them on their lives and sharing mine. I liked the participants in the workshops and felt I was doing a good job.

On the morning of the third day of the seminar, I was descending three flights of marble stairs when my foot slipped and I tumbled down from the top. I can still experience the dreadful speed of the fall. The speed was more terrifying than the pain. At times, I felt as though I were flying, and at other times, I was crashing against the stairs. I fell onto a marble floor and woke up with friends asking me what hurt. I was confused and couldn't put words together in any coherent fashion. Every part of my body hurt.

I'm thinking... "Where am I? What happened? What is the terrible sound I hear in my head? What are you saying to me?" I'm confused and very frightened. I can't move. "Why can't I? FALL...FALL...I FELL! Please help me." I was hurt and bleeding. I needed help.

My friends comforted me and told me help was on the way. They kept talking to me and slowly, I began to understand them.

At the hospital, I had various tests and was told that my ear was almost severed from my head. The doctors sewed it back on. I had a torn achilles tendon and could not walk. More importantly, I was told I had a closed head injury and that my brain had experienced severe trauma. While the doctors were talking to me, it was all I could do to understand them. The voices around me were muffled. I tried to stay awake but I felt so sleepy that keeping my eyes open was a challenge. I tried to understand what had happened to me. Something very major had happened to me and I struggled to comprehend it.

"What did all of this mean? What did I need to do to make myself normal again?"

I tried to say that I needed to go back to work, but I was unable to make myself understood. I tried several times, but my friends said, "No...no ...not today. You can't go to work today."

After some time in the hospital, I stayed at my friends' home and the doctor came daily to check on me. I had a ferocious headache which refused to go away. My vision was extremely fuzzy and when people spoke to me, it was as though I was at the end of a very long tunnel. Worse yet, I failed to comprehend what they were saying to me. I was so grateful to my friends, Antoinette and Salamon, for looking after me during this time.

I kept thinking, "I want to go home. I want to be near my family. What will I do?" I was unable to travel because flying would increase brain swelling. After several weeks, I finally returned home, a very different person.

I had major problems that I knew would impact my ability to work, but I was alive! I was having difficulty communicating; the doctors called it aphasia. Understanding what people were saying to me and coherently responding were issues I grappled with at each interaction. I couldn't read! I loved to read…I was a "lector" at church. I had been a regular reader but now I couldn't read, so I had to withdraw from this ministry. I hoped it would not be a long-term withdrawal. My life experience was changing dramatically.

I felt so dispirited and discouraged. I was finally in a place where I could continue the work I loved, and now I don't think I can process what is going on around me. What will I do if my brain is severely damaged? How will I work? What kind of a mother or grandmother will I be? Will I be able to make sense of things? I've come back from bad situations before; I have to do so now. I have to find a more positive outlook. Maybe I need to focus on that: I am alive and I'm happy for that. I can come out of this. I'm a survivor.

I managed to make it home. Sara was shocked and frightened, but in spite of how she felt, she was there for me. She took care of me, took me to doctors, saw to it that I had food and was there when I needed to cry. She reassured me when I doubted myself. She was my strength.

Could I continue to work as a therapist? After several months of recuperating, I was once again able to speak coherently. I thought I sounded as I had prior to the accident. I thought I would see some clients and see how I felt about myself as a therapist. In the therapy session, something was dramatically different. Before my accident, when working as a therapist, I had always relied on empathy…being able to sense the client's state of being. This was a very physical feeling that almost felt like our minds were spliced together. Working as a therapist used to feel like a spiritual experience that led me to a clear understanding of my client's issues. This visceral sense of being able to feel and understand what others were trying to tell me was gone. My affect felt flat. Before my accident, I knew what people felt… what they were experiencing…even what they had confronted in the past. Clients reported that they had been understood as never before. Now, I didn't know what others felt or what I felt. I failed to comprehend the struggles my clients were dealing with. As a client was telling me his issues and what he wanted to resolve in his life, I had a sense that I wanted to slap him and say, "Wake up and smell the roses…get on with life…you only pass this moment once…make use of it." Good advice, but not good for someone beginning to sort out his life experience. I could not do therapy with this simplistic approach to serious issues.

I was still dealing with achilles tendon surgery, and decided I had tried to return to work too soon. It had only been one month since my accident. I gave myself more time to recuperate. My short experience back in the therapy room made me fearful that I should not be doing therapy again. I'd not been able to get a picture of my client…what were his issues…what did he want to deal with…was he suicidal? I couldn't figure out what I was dealing with. I needed more time…maybe a lot more time. Did I have the capacity to work as a psychotherapist and safely treat my clients? Had my antennae for serious issues been damaged in my fall? I loved my work.

Working as a psychotherapist has been exciting for me. I loved helping individuals in pain overcome that pain. At the moment, I was the person in pain, and I had no idea how to help myself. Ceasing work as a psychotherapist was painful for me, but I thought it would only be a few months. I was wrong. I thought I would very quickly regain my skills and be my old self again. I was wrong. I grieved the loss, but I knew I could not afford to wallow in pity for myself. I had a lot of work ahead of me if I was to continue to have a meaningful life. I had to plot a new direction for my life. What worthwhile work could I do if I could not be a psychotherapist?

I felt as though my immediate roadmap for life was full of roadblocks and dead ends. I was depressed, tired, and found it hard to get moving in the morning; however, I knew I needed to find the strength to move on. I had always been bursting with energy and now I was numb and silent. I reminded myself that I had been through physical trauma before when I broke my neck and I managed to move on. At this point, I wasn't even sure what "move on" meant. I was used to my brain and my verbal skills being the prime movers of my success. At this point, I knew that my verbal skills were more limited than at any other time in my life experience. The ability to be genuinely empathetic was not within my grasp. I felt like I couldn't think my way out of a paper bag.

I was grateful that Sara, Kurdt, and my friends were there for me. They supported me and were patient with me when I stumbled. Sara, in particular, was amazing. I decided to close my psychotherapy practice permanently. My work had been of utmost importance in my life and I could not function now…I closed my practice…I have no idea whether or not I will ever again be able to do the work I love. I cried and I also felt terrified…what could I do?

I went to a neurologist and was told that I needed rehab for my head injury. I agreed, but I didn't have the money or the insurance coverage for the program he suggested, since I was not part of a group insurance plan. The coverage I had would cover only a very short stint in a rehab program. I was fortunate that I had taken out a disability insurance plan when I adopted my children. It was one of those "just in case" kinds of insurance. The hope was that I would never need to use it. At this point, however, I needed to use it and I was grateful for it. I was thankful that I had worked in neurology for a short time, and I had a sense of what the program I needed would look like. In the meantime, I hoped that my various skills would return. I was frightened. I had always thought that I would remain a therapist forever. I surmised that even as I aged and if physical movement became an issue, I would always have my brain. I had never imagined, in my wildest dreams, that anything could happen to my brain. This was not supposed to happen. It was not a part of my agenda.

Throughout this ordeal, Sara remained by my side. She took me to all of my doctor appointments, to rehab, to church, and to anything I needed. She helped me make major decisions as I was doubtful of my judgment. She did the grocery shopping and the cooking. I can't believe how wonderful and how loving she was. She seemed to understand what the loss of my work meant for me. I don't know what I would have done without her. Kurdt came and was helpful, but he lived a distance away and Sara was willing to take on whatever was needed. I was so grateful to Sara. She understood what this injury to my brain had done to me, and she stood ready to help me. She knew my needs.

This was probably one of the lowest points in my life. I was depressed. I didn't know what to do to make my world better. I wasn't used to "needing" others and self-sufficiency was the rule I lived by. I needed to learn how to accept help from others. I had to stop being angry with myself for being needy. I had to accept the "new Me." I had to learn who this new "Me" was and I also needed to assess her skills. In order to get to know "Me" and accept "Me," I had to rid myself of the mantle of shame I wore so willingly. I had done nothing shameful. Having disabilities was nothing to be ashamed of. I needed a program designed to help me recuperate. The first step in that program was to accept my injuries, disabilities, and the fact that I was no longer the brightest person in the room.

MY PROGRAM

I set up a program for myself. The first step for me was applying for disability insurance and social security disability. I qualified for these programs. I actually felt embarrassed when applying, because this was proof that I was now inferior and damaged. I kept telling myself that I would soon be better and would not need help. My money worries were taken care of, so I began work on my rehabilitation program. I tried to work for 6 or 8 hours daily on memory, reading, and balance exercises. I worked on everything I could find that might stretch my brain.

I joined a stock group and learned how to evaluate stocks. This involved inputting information, remembering long lists of numbers, and making decisions with respect to stocks based on the information I had gathered. I then had to present the stocks I recommended to the stock group. That was difficult as it meant talking and supporting my recommendations. This was very different from what I had been doing in the past, but I felt I was learning and progressing. Although I had never been good with numbers, I decided I might have found another interesting line of work.

I couldn't believe the sound of my own voice. "Who was this?" I sounded so hesitant; the power had gone out of me. I had to get to know myself all over again. I needed to find strength and I had to learn how to project it. This task seemed insurmountable but I had to succeed.

I worked hard on learning to read out loud again. I practiced by myself, reading everything aloud, taping my reading, and listening to my words. I then corrected words I felt I hadn't said accurately. I wanted to go back to church and become a reader again. After 6 months or so, the aphasia was less of a problem for me and I decided to try to read in church. I actually did okay. I wasn't wonderful, but people could understand me. I continued to read and got better and better. At the same time, I had read that singing is great for the brain, so I joined a choir at church. This was wonderful as I quickly learned the music and the words.

I had lost what had felt like magic to me when I worked with people in my practice, but I gained some other skills. I missed the excitement of the work I had done in the past. I missed traveling. I missed all of the friends I had made throughout the world in the years of my international work. I missed myself…the person I had been. I had trouble recognizing the "new" me. I did mourn my losses and there were many. However, even though I had lost valued abilities, I gained others. It was so important for me to remain positive. As I struggled, I was afraid that depression might become an outcome of all of this trauma. I decided that it could not and would not be an outcome for me. I would grieve my losses, but I would not stay there and wallow in pain…I had to get up and move and face the new day. Every day was a new chance to learn something exciting.

I was fortunate that I was again given a wondrous gift…my first grandchild, Alex. I could not believe my happiness. Kurdt and Kelly had their first child, and he was absolutely beautiful. They were so excited. Suddenly, my life was again full and again exciting. It was a different excitement, but it felt very good. I wasn't lauded by a large audience, but it was wonderful to look into the smiling eyes of a very little one.

I have many gaps in my memory and still have some deficits, but I am very happy with my recovery. I still panic near the stairs and often feel the speed of that fall in my mind and body. I still have nightmares where I again experience falling downstairs. These nightmares seem to blend with dreams of my life during WWII. However, I am so thankful to God for my family. I am grateful that I am alive and ready to continue to be an important influence on Sara and Kurdt and their families.

I had gotten used to being "the star," and I had begun to enjoy the praise that came my way. It seemed strange that accolades now came for my progress with a head injury, not for the quality of my work as a therapist. I wanted more of myself and for myself. I felt shame when I sought out words that did not come with the facility to which I had become accustomed.

Accepting the "new" me was not easy. I mourned the loss of the work I loved. I had always been exceedingly busy and now I actually had time on my hands. How do I make each moment count? I worked hard at keeping my spirits up, as it was so easy to sink into despair, and I knew that letting depression take hold of me would not be good. I wrote down daily affirmations, a reminder to focus on the good. I set out weekly goals, and worked on accomplishing them. I did everything I could think of to keep my positive attitude, and slowly, I felt myself "rising from the ashes of the mess I had been in. While in my twenties, I had experienced a terrible accident where my neck was broken, and I had not been successful in escaping depression. I had promised myself at the time that I would never again sink that low, and I had kept that promise.

I was grateful that I lived in town and didn't need to go far for my everyday needs. My life was changing daily, and I loved the changes. Gradually, after about six months, I began to drive again and experienced no major issues. I felt like my vision and coordination were not a problem for me.

SARA AND GERRY

Sara came to me with news…she was going to get married. She met Gerry shortly after breaking up with the young man she had lived with. She expressed some urgency when it came to the marriage date, as she told me that she was about three months pregnant. She spoke of two major problems: Gerry's family did not approve of her. They had never met; however, they decided that since Sara was Hispanic, the marriage would not work. He was supposed to marry a Phillipino girl. They thought Sara was a "golddigger" and refused to accept her. Sara hoped that, in time, they would get to know her and welcome her. This did not happen. Gerry did not confront his parents' behavior and as a result, his family chose to have no contact with Sara or the grandchildren born of this union. This neglect has continued to this day and has been painful for Sara and her children.

The second problem was much simpler and involved Gerry's house. Sara said the place was in terrible condition and she could never live in it in its present state. She cried as she told me about the home. "It's a disaster, Mom!" I knew that the first thing I needed to do was take a good look at it.

I saw Gerry's house and it **was** a disaster. It needed everything and then some. Gerry was a packrat, and his home was filled with boxes still sealed from previous moves. There were narrow paths in the home to go from room to room, and there was no place to sit down. In some places, the boxes were piled ceiling height. There were also places where any space available was filled with items he had picked up as freebies along the road. He even had a very old and very rusted barber chair. He apparently kept telling himself that he could fix these things when he had some time. I saw a few redeeming features in the freebies. As I tried one appliance after another, I quickly discovered that nothing worked. Even the refrigerator did not work. The electrical system and the plumbing needed help. I was still recovering from my head injury, but I thought I could help. I really understood what Sara meant when she said she could not live there and she couldn't bring a baby into a home as dangerous as this one. I told Sara that she and her fiance had a choice: they could have a big wedding or I could renovate their home. They both said, "the house," and Gerry even agreed not to interfere with the project or even to look at anything until I said it was done. He asked, "Does it include throwing things away?" I said "yes," and he still agreed to let me do the job.

Kurdt invited Gerry to go fishing for a weekend and he happily agreed to go. My first task was to hire Honeymoon Haulers to get rid of the colossal amount of junk that stood in the way of the work we needed to do. I assembled a crew, observed the demolition, got rid of all of the junk, ordered the appliances, cabinets, windows, and so much more and we were underway. The first thing I had the crew assemble was the storage shed now occupying the backyard. All of the boxes quickly found a home in the shed, and now we had a house we could take apart and fix. I was amazed that I could organize a project as complex as this. This undertaking was actually good therapy for me.

Gerry came home from the fishing trip and screamed: "What happened to my stuff? You took my stuff!"

"Gerry, don't you remember that you gave me permission to do the necessary work to get this place in order and functioning? Your boxes are in the shed, but the other junk is gone, as is the refuse from the demolition. You need to look at some of this other stuff and decide what needs to be junked."

Gerry was shaken up and grumbled for a while. He complained that he had that stuff for a long time. He was getting ready to get rid of it, but he wasn't ready.

It took almost two months, but by the wedding day, the house was finished. Sara was married, moved into a fully functioning house, and her baby boy was born.

Sara, Gerry, and I met at the hospital when her contractions began, but Gerry decided he was having a cardiac event, and ended up going to the emergency room rather than obstetrics. Sara and I walked up and down the corridors of the hospital, trying to get the baby to turn for an optimum delivery. The doctors said the baby was in a breech position. Sara took charge and told everyone to be quiet while she changed her position in the bed. I couldn't believe it, but the baby was ready, no longer breech. I got to cut the baby's cord…what an honor. Gerry, in the meantime, suffered his way through his victim role and missed the birth of his first child. The doctors at the ER found nothing wrong with him.

I now had two wonderful grandchildren; however, Alex lived a considerable distance away. I connected with Kurdt's family whenever I could, and I was glad that they had Kelly's large family and that they were also excited about the new addition to the family. I was happy that Sara allowed me to be an integral part of Anthony's life from the very beginning. Luckily, their house was a very short drive for me. Gerry continued to compete for attention and he also continued his hoarding behavior.

After several years, Sara and Gerry moved to a much larger new home in Pittsfield Township. Matthew was born when Anthony was two years old, followed by Natalie and Christina, all about two years apart. They are a lively, creative and exciting group of very active children. I saw them daily and looked after them when Sara was at work. When preschool began for Anthony, he stayed at my house during the week so that I could take him to school and pick him up. I didn't quite understand this routine, but it worked for my schedule. I believed that Sara had a reason to ask that I do this, and I loved every minute of it.

A FULL HOUSE

My house was quiet, at least at night. In the daytime, Sara and the kids visited daily

and we played in the park and had many picnics. At one time, Kurdt and his family moved in as Kelly had a new job as an occupational therapist and Kurdt was attending community college. They lived in the walkout lower level and stayed for about two years. Alex was beginning to display some of the signs of a major problem. I suspected Autism was the issue, but no one else was willing to consider this diagnosis. Finally, when Alex was about three years old, the family physician spoke to them about what they dreaded to hear…Alex was on the Autism spectrum. From that time on, however, Kurdt and Kelly learned everything they could about the problems plaguing their son. They became experts on Autism, working constantly with Alex. Their hard work paid off since he's now a bright, engaging young man. His differences are now charming. Kurdt and Kelly were wanting more space and were in a position to purchase their own home. I had started working as a Realtor, and showed them a variety of homes. They found a small home on a large lot in Pinckney. They bought it and have raised their four children in this home.

With my downstairs now free, I began to rent the space out. My first tenant was a mom and a teen daughter. The next was a couple. They rented until they had a child and then sought a larger space. I thought the lower level was again mine to play in. The rental income was a great help to me.

I was bored, and I really wanted to do something useful with my life. I also needed to make some money. The disability insurance I had stopped contributing to my welfare when I turned 65. I wanted a job, but one where I could generally set my schedule and basically be my own boss again. In 2004, I got the training and passed the state exam for Realtor. The training consisted of 40 classroom hours, followed by the state exam. I discovered that real estate is not for dummies…it is not a simple process. Completing a sale requires a good deal of thought and a good awareness of people and the law. A good Realtor needs to know how to read critically, and also needs to remember a good deal of math. Much of the math I learned in grade school, but now I knew that there was a use for it. I learned that when people are selling or looking for a new home, they are not necessarily reasonable. They often think their home is worth much more than it's appraised for. When they are in the market for a new home, they often insist the home they want is overpriced and wonder why I can't get the seller to reduce the price. Some people insist they don't need an inspection, complain when I ask them to sign off on it, and complain after closing about all of the problems the house has. In some ways, this world is not much different from the psychotherapeutic world.

I now had another profession. The neat thing about this job was that it gave me permission to look at lots of houses. I had always enjoyed seeing how people designed and organized their homes. Now, I got to look inside. I learned how to appraise, market, and finally sell homes. I started in my neighborhood…I saw it as my "farm". This neighborhood was fairly new, built beginning in 1994. I moved into my house in 1996. I was elected to the condo board after moving in, and I've been part of that board ever since. I "SOLD" My neighborhood! I knew the houses, I knew the rules, I knew the people, and I did a great job with each listing. This was supposed to be a temporary job…until I felt I could again do a good job as a therapist. I was still praying to get my skills back. I continued this job until 2024. It was perfect for me at the time. Thank you, God.

A HOUSE FULL OF LAUGHTER AND LOVE

In 2004, Sara left Gerry. She and the 4 children moved in with me one evening when she had enough. Hoarding had been a lifelong obsession with Gerry, and he had also begun abusing the boys. Sara finally had her fill of him. She and the children were done. The day before they moved into my home, the couple in the basement and Jim, the upstairs tenant, all moved out. Sara had apparently been thinking about moving for quite a while, and when my house was empty, she stood at the door with the four kids and the clothes on their backs and asked to stay. She simply said that her house had become unlivable. I asked no questions, but welcomed them. There were many issues in Sara's marriage and the total rejection from Gerry's parents was a constant ache. It was late in the evening and we would talk the next day.

Sara and the kids had brought nothing, so I tried to get some of their clothing and toys, but Gerry refused me entry to the house. "They are all my things…I paid for them," he said. I tried to talk to him, but he was adamant. Several days later, Sara used her key to enter the house so that she could get clothes for herself and the kids. She also gathered up some of their favorite toys. She managed to take a few items, but most of their possessions were still in the house.

Gerry called, furious, "That was my stuff you took. You broke into My house…you have to give me back my stuff."

Sara exclaimed: "But Gerry…I didn't break in…I had my keys…the clothes belong to the kids and me. The Barbie I took was Natalie's…we gave them to the kids after we bought them. The toys were Christmas presents. None of this is yours. My dresses are mine!"

Gerry continued to argue and insist that since he had paid for the items, they were all his. Sara gave up on the argument. I think she decided it wasn't worth the fight, and she was also worried that Gerry might retaliate. He had a very bad temper and could be very unreasonable. She was happy to be away from all of the junk Gerry had collected on a daily basis and she was grateful for the peace our home provided.

The home I was living in at the time Sara and the kids moved in was new as of 1996. It was the house that followed the home that was sinking. It was a ranch home with a walkout basement that was also finished. The downstairs opened onto a city park that had tennis courts, play stations, swings, woods, and a lot of green space that I didn't have to mow myself. The home, however, was much smaller than any of my previous homes. I ended up with 3 bedrooms and 2 baths upstairs, and 2 bedrooms and a bath downstairs with a downstairs living room and kitchen. I finished almost one hundred percent of the house. We had to do a bit of squeezing together…the boys shared a large bedroom downstairs and the girls shared a downstairs bedroom. They all shared the downstairs bathroom and learned how to take turns. When the kids became teens, I lost my office, which I wasn't really using, and it became a bedroom for Matthew. When the kids began high school, we were within walking distance. The good thing about this house is that we were close to everything we could want or need.

The children took this change in their lives in stride. Thankfully, they were very familiar with my home as most evenings and weekends had been spent there. They enjoyed the park and the neighborhood. They were also closer to St. Francis School, and often stayed for after-school activities. They were involved in art projects and musical theater, and all became violinists as they entered kindergarten.

Gerry was invited to be a part of the kids' lives, and he came to occasional concerts. He seldom called for birthdays. He came for the holidays when we invited him.

As for me, my life was again full of energy, the sounds of children, and the hope embodied in young lives. I felt so alive. I had never been so grateful for the gift of life. I was busy with one activity after another, all of which brought me joy. I had trained to be a Realtor, and I began to earn a living again. The great thing about this job is the flexibility of my time. I let the kids be my priority, and if an appointment interfered with a commitment to the kids, I canceled the appointment. I had been too involved with work when Sara and Kurdt were children, and I did not want to repeat that mistake with this crew.

I was amazed at the life I was living…I had the family I had always longed for. The time with my children had gone so swiftly. We had a mixture of wonderful times and hard times. I blinked and they had grown up and married. Now, I could join in the lives of another generation and savor every minute of their energy-filled growth experience. I couldn't imagine being happier.

LIFE WITH CHILDREN

I never imagined that the world could provide such richness. The four children that Sara brought to my home in the middle of the night opened up enlivening, stimulating, unbelievable and wonderful years for me. Children are so REAL and they expect TRUTH. They want adults to be true to them in what they say and do. There is such a complicated simplicity in their dealings with others. I learned so much from these four and I continue to learn from them. The two children I adopted taught me a great deal, but many of those teachings were painful. We struggled, and our love for each other helped us come to resolutions. Living with my grandchildren was fun and so enlightening. Every day was new and brought something exciting. I loved the noise in the home…and the quiet when all were asleep.

I was a significant part of these children's lives twenty-four hours per day. I became the photographer for the school, put together two church directories, and, best of all, joined the elementary school violin group. The teacher invited any parent who brought a child to participate if they wanted, and boy…was I ever ready. I was the only person who took her up on this offer. I felt silly sitting on the risers with a group of little kids. We sounded absolutely terrible but the group did get better. I did not. It took a while for me to get over my embarrassment. To add insult to injury, we had to participate in a recital. I couldn't believe it. Here I was, standing up on a stage with a bunch of little kids who could play our piece…in fact, some even had it memorized. I couldn't do it, but I did my best rendition of the piece while playing my "air violin". (the hair on my bow never touched the strings…and thank God for that). I did survive that recital. I do know that Anthony was not thrilled with my presence in the group, but he didn't complain. From my vantage point, he seemed to like it, and I had fun. I was probably the most inept pupil the teacher had to deal with. My fine motor coordination had never really recovered from the fall, but that didn't matter to me. I tried…I worked at it…and I loved being a part of that funny young group of kids who were working at something. Some were willing participants…others felt like prisoners forced to suffer…but ultimately, we had fun. I played "air violin" for about a year but then decided that my talents were probably more needed when it came to controlling the behavior of the young virtuosos in the group. So…I became the "principal" of the group. I was involved with this group for at least eleven years. What a trip. All four of our gang were a part of this group over the course of many years.

We spent many hours on soccer fields with all of the kids and time at regattas with our rowing team members, Anthony and Natalie. The boys spent endless days and weekends at Boy Scout events. Sara loved going to the camp outings and helped enormously at these events. Christina grew to love ultimate frisbee; however, COVID curbed her ability to enjoy the games as most were canceled. All of the kids were in Orchestra or Band and were accomplished musicians. I got vicarious pleasure watching them perform, whether in concerts or taking them to practice with their teachers. I loved helping Matthew apply and get accepted to the Blue Lake Symphonic Band as they traveled to Europe for a month. He was only twelve years old, but he said the trip changed his life.

I was able to take the children on their first airplane trips. We went to Atlanta to visit their Aunt Corrie. What fun! We created a memory book of each trip which consisted of the kid's observations of what we saw and who we met. We took photos of people, places and things, and had them developed immediately so we could put them in the correct spot in the book. I also took driving trips with them, the longest being a month-long trip to Idaho with Anthony. I took 9-year-old Anthony on this venture and he was my navigator. We were initially going to camp all the way, but after the first night, I decided that my body was now better suited for a motel room. We stopped and saw all of the wonderful sites along the way. We went caving at the Wind River caverns, hiked some in the badlands, saw the corn palace, enjoyed Jackson Hole, the geysers in Yellowstone and the vastness of the scrublands. In Idaho, we stayed with my friend, Marcia in Idaho, and visited the Sacajewa center, bathed in hot springs, and observed a lot of wildlife. He also was able to raft on the Idaho River. Anthony really got into this trip. He handled the maps and made decisions concerning what routes we would take and had many ideas as to what we would stop and see. On the way, we played all of the Harry Potter books on the radio and we had several other audiobooks of this sort. What a wonderful time.

I took other trips with the kids. I drove Anthony to Space Camp in Huntsville, Alabama, as he won scholarships and spent time there over two summers. Matthew came along, and we drove to Atlanta while Anthony was at camp. We were able to explore Atlanta and enjoyed staying with Corrie until we picked Anthony up from camp. We then continued our trip to include South Carolina and the East Coast, especially Washington. We visited with the kids' uncle Angel and his family and stayed in their beautiful home. We saw many exciting historical sites, including the very places where slaves were sold, many grand old homes, and the Atlantic Ocean. The boys were quite interested in all of the Smithsonian museums, especially the Aerospace and the Spy museums. Matthew really enjoyed the subways in Washington and the various places we could play video games. We stayed at the Mayflower Hotel. It was a lovely place right in the middle of everything. We had various incidents each night: The room was not available until it was VERY late; the hotel did not charge for the room and paid for our dinner. The second night, Matthew got a shock when trying to plug something in and the hotel again gave us a free night. On the third night, a number of things went wrong, including a loud alarm…again a free night. We never even had to complain…they just volunteered the free nights. Wow…I didn't expect that. God is good.

The girls and I took trips to Atlanta to visit Corrie and Chris and again, we were treated royally. One of the most exciting car trips I took with the girls included my friend Elaine and her granddaughter, Annika. We visited schools in Pennsylvania and New Jersey, including Princeton. The kids enjoyed the Crayola and Hershey factories and they even seemed to enjoy our accounts of the history of the area. We went to Elaine's hometown and she got to show these very interested children some of her old haunts, including her boarding school. They were fascinated by her stories, and I have to admit that I also was. We then went to Gettysburg and were fortunate to have an expert in the area give us a tour. We decided not to do the midnight tour of the ghosts of Gettysburg, as I was concerned about nightmares and we still had 9 days of our trip to go. We saw many of the battlefields and learned much more about the Civil War. After leaving Gettysburg, we were off to Washington, where we explored all of the Smithsonian museums. It was insufferably hot in Washington, so we did not spend much time outdoors and walking to various sites was challenging enough. We were fortunate to be able to stay at a friend's home, and that made our trip more relaxed and definitely less expensive. The kids were great travelers and low on complaints.

I spent no time wallowing over losses. Falling down the stairs in Belgium became part of my past that I chose not to dwell on. I am grateful for this. I guess I believe that when one road closes down, another is opening and can lead to wonderful things. I accepted the dramatic changes in my life and have seldom looked back. I do miss my work as a therapist. I truly loved working with people as they sorted out their lives. It was a privilege. Sometimes, I wish that my grandkids could see who I was when I traveled, spoke in front of groups, and did some of the dramatic therapeutic work I was known for. I am continuously coming to terms with my life. I'm no longer a STAR, but a much loved GRANDMA…AKA …G-WOMAN.

PROBLEMS OF THE HEART

Around Thanksgiving time 2014, I traveled to Corrie's house in Atlanta for a visit. Overall, family life at home was moving along quite well. I continued having fun with Sara and the kids. Everyone was doing what they needed to be doing. Two of the kids were in High School and two were in middle school, and all were into music and their studies. Everything on the homefront was gliding along smoothly. I hated to miss our Thanksgiving at home, but for some unknown reason, it seemed like a good time to visit with my sister. We have always been close and stay connected with daily telephone calls. We love our daily talks, and are very supportive of one another. We usually have in-person visits once or twice per year, and really look forward to these visits. For some reason, I wanted to be with her. I felt I needed her support.

I hadn't been feeling well for some time, but hadn't said anything to Corrie or the family at home. I had been feeling tired, out of breath, and weak, but during this trip to Atlanta, I really felt I had major issues. When I landed in Atlanta, one of my biggest hurdles was simply getting through the airport. I was lightheaded, gasping for breath and hurting all over. I had to stop at least four times to sit down and gather my strength and my breath before moving on to finally get to the luggage area where Corrie and Chris would meet me. I don't recall ever feeling as weak as I did at that time. I was afraid I would collapse. I thought some rest would help me, but things did not improve. I knew something was terribly wrong. At her home, Corrie and I tried to go on a short walk, but I barely made it back. I knew I was in trouble.

Concerned, Corrie asked: "You have to promise me that you will see your doctor when you get home. I know you don't like to see doctors, but please, do it for me."

Meekly, I said: "I promise. I know this is important. I'm scared, too."

I saw my doctor and was instantly referred to a cardiologist. I was immediately scheduled for a stress test. I got hooked up to the instruments and began the test. Moments into the first test, the doctors stopped everything. Apparently, the ultrasound images showed that my heart was not going to tolerate even the easy part of the stress test. The doctor said the problems I was having were related to the valves in my heart. I needed open heart surgery to replace the aortic valve and repair others. It was supposed to be a simple procedure and I was told I would be out of the hospital in three day

. I had surgery the day before Christmas and it sounds like anything that could possibly have gone wrong went wrong. I woke up three weeks later in the intensive care unit very confused and weak. I had almost died. The aortic valve they had prepared to replace mine was the wrong size, and they had to find another one that would fit. They also had to repair the mitral valve and unblock two arteries. I was on the heart-lung machine for double the recommended time. It is a miracle that my brain was not damaged, and that the only organ in my body damaged was my kidney. All that I remember of this time is that I experienced frightening nightmares. I also had an experience or a dream that I vividly remember. The dream follows.

I'm with Mama and I'm about five years old. We're in our garden in Lokeren and this is the safest, best place in the world. Mama has

to clean the sore on my arm. The doctor said it was blood poisoning and she has to rub it with something that hurts a lot. I don't want her to do it because it hurts so much. Mama tells me that she has to do it but that she has a job for me that is very hard. "While I do this, I want you to think about offering your pain up to God. Do you think you can do that?" I said, "yes". She helped me pray and it did help my pain. Then she seemed to change, and she told me: "I know you probably want to stay with me right now, but you can't; you need to return to your family. It's not your time. The kids still need you. Your time will come, but not now. The dream disappeared and I felt pain.

I remember waking up very sad and terrified. It was as though I was trapped in a Star Trek episode and I had been captured by the Borg. I looked down at my body and saw four huge drains in my chest and an assortment of wires and tubes. I was utterly confused. "Was this real? What was going on? Where was I? Where was Mama? Where did she go?" I couldn't move my body. That was probably the most terrifying part of this experience. "What happened to me?"

Most of this information about what happened to me during and post-surgery came after I left the hospital. I would not bet on its accuracy. I was very sick. I stayed in intensive care for another two weeks and then went into rehab. My road back was long and painful. I have never been a good patient. Being a good patient means giving up control. I have a limited capacity for patience. I had to learn how to stand up. I had to learn how to walk. I do not like feeling weak. It frightens me. Using a walker and a wheelchair felt demeaning to me. I thought they defined me as a cripple, as someone who is disabled. I wanted out of rehab as soon as possible. I put up such a fight about this that I think I was probably discharged too soon.

Both Sara and Kurdt were amazing throughout this ordeal. Sara was particularly incredible. She stayed with me all the time while I was in intensive care, only going home to make sure all was okay with the kids. She even got Gerry to spend several nights at the hospital. The kids all said they were terrified. I feel sad that I had no awareness of the help I got. I don't even remember the friends who came and visited and prayed for me. Needing and accepting help was not my strong suit, but I got help in spite of myself. Once I woke up, I couldn't even get in or out of bed without help from a staff person. I learned how to do all of the things I needed to do. I learned how to get out of bed, how to use the toilet, how to take steps (one at a time), how to walk with a walker, how to dress myself, and the list goes on. I was down. I was really down. Could I come back from this experience? The kids really needed me. Sara needed me. If I won't come out of this for myself, I have to make myself do what I need to do for them.

The depression I felt was deeper than what I had ever felt before in my life. The difference was that I knew I would not hurt myself or kill myself as a way of escaping the pain. I had made this contract with myself and I knew I would keep it no matter how bad things were in my life. I was trapped in a body racked with pain and I needed to learn how to rely on others to help me deal with everything I could not do for myself. I prayed that I would find the inner strength to willingly accept and appreciate the help others gave me so freely. God was providing me with more opportunities to learn about pride. Was I too proud to accept help for my disabilities?

When I was finally released from rehab, I could walk a couple of steps with a walker and then I needed to sit down. In spite of my weakened condition, I decided I needed to start work. Yes…work.

Actually, I had started up again while I was in rehab. I took a listing that sold instantly. With the help of people in my office and a good telephone line, the sale went through. Wow…I thought…I can do this. Everything had gone so smoothly that I believed I could work as I had before my surgery. I was still refusing to face reality.

I needed to show some potential clients homes in Ann Arbor. I had no idea how to do this as I still could not walk ten feet. Thank God I could still talk…and I did talk. I am grateful that my friend, Janetta, agreed to help me. I decided I could drive…yes…drive…I would drive Janetta and the clients to the houses they wanted to see, and Janetta would open the homes and show the inside of the homes. I would stay in the car. What a relief. I didn't even have to get out of the car. I could not have walked to the front doors of the houses and climbing stairs was impossible. It was nuts! Everyone knew it was nuts. The clients were very nice and didn't even question this crazy system. They politely went along with the display of strength I was trying to present. I did not see these clients again, but I was grateful for everyone's patience. Once at my home again, it took me forever to get out of the car, even with help. I had come face to face with the reality that recovery would take time and that I was in the early stages. I still can't believe that I got my friend involved in such a crazy stunt. I was so grateful to Janetta for helping me through these painful early days of my recovery.

However, a stunt like the one with Janetta was taking a risk and jeopardizing my safety and the safety of others, and not the wisest thing to do. I decided to wait a while to return to work. I did very little work during the next few months, but at least I knew I could work (with some help) if I had to. I suppose that my stubborn insistence that "I can do it, I don't need help" and an occasional "thank you" actually spurred me on in my recovery. I put all of my energy into restoring my strength. I think my family was happy to finally get me out of the house. When I could do more for myself and when I felt more freedom, I was a nicer person.

Sara and the kids were very worried, and also very helpful. The kids knew I was an important person when it came to providing stability in their lives. They also knew that the person needing stability now was me. They helped me with my rehab at every step of the way. They yelled at me when I was resistant to doing the exercises I needed to do. They encouraged me and loved me. I was grumpy; I couldn't cook meals, clean the house, do laundry or work at my job. I knew I needed to earn some money to pay the bills, but I certainly didn't look the part of an experienced Realtor. I wanted to get back to work and ultimately, I did return.

This time of my life was a time of deep soul-searching and contemplation. I had more time on my hands than I had ever had before. I learned a lot about being human with human needs. I learned a good deal about humility. In the past, pride had kept me from accepting the help that was offered and needed. I had experienced suffering before, but I felt this was my "most real" experience with pain and even death. I somehow decided to let each moment have its own special magic. I worked on looking for the good that might have come from this experience. This felt like a stretch, but I knew I needed to think positively. I was learning how to accept and deal with issues that I was not in charge of. I thankfully discovered that the world did not collapse or stop when I was not in charge. I kept myself out of the depression that I feared and focused on accepting the positive in my experience. I had so much to be grateful for. I had Sara and Kurdt and their kids. I had many friends.

I had my life and another chance to deal with the issues I had not yet resolved. I was still intact.

I found it fascinating that the problems that grounded me were issues of the heart. The heart is the symbol of love and connection and although I fiercely felt love for my children, grandchildren, Corrie and my family, I had my share of difficulties taking in the love that came to me. Accepting love from others means letting your guard down, and opening your heart up to others. It was interesting that I could tell Corrie that she deserved good things and that she didn't need to panic when someone was good to her and did things for her and at the same time not grant this for myself. Opening up means letting others see me with all my warts. And love me with all of my warts. I learned that there were needs I couldn't fulfill on my own. I really needed others. This was not something I could get an advanced degree in and solve. I felt in many ways like I had been broken, but I felt happy. It was now late Spring 2015.

DEAD?????

I was in a lengthy recovery from serious and scary heart surgery, but I was finally able to resume some semblance of life separated from illness, and had even decided to attempt a very limited shopping trip. I was going to buy myself something new. I was not ready for the bombshell that awaited me. What happened to me during this time was totally unexpected. When I was finally able to go to a store and hopefully buy something, I got the shock of my life. I'd had more than my share of "shocks," but this one really left me confused. I found a wonderful blouse; it fit perfectly, was the color I loved, and I wanted it. I took out my credit card in order to pay for the item.

"I'm sorry, but this card is declined…do you have another card?"

In fact, I had a number of cards, and I willingly offered one after another, only to have each declined in turn.

"What could be wrong?" I asked.

"If I were you, I would go to my bank and find out…you say you haven't used these cards in months…something must be going on."

I went to my bank, and found out that all of my charge accounts had all been closed. In fact, my checking and my savings accounts were also closed.

"Why are they closed? I had no balance on the cards," I asked plaintively.

"You better sit down for this…according to the information I have here, you are dead. Someone apparently declared you dead," said the bank manager.

I started to laugh, as I had difficulty believing what I was hearing. "I'm alive…I'm here…I'm breathing…I'm talking." My voice got louder and more shrill as I was inundated with feelings which overwhelmed me. I put my head in my hands and bent over in a useless effort to calm myself. "What do I do now?" I felt tears come to my eyes and roll down my face.

"I don't really know," said the manager. "I've never had to deal with this before.

Go and find out who declared you dead and you will have to find proof that you are alive.

I walked out of the bank, stunned. I had just experienced a life-death issue with my heart surgery, and now I was dealing with a situation that directly contradicted my experience of reality. "I know I'm alive…I need to prove it to the powers that be when it comes to my finances. Where do I start?" As I thought about my situation, I decided to start with the hospital where I had my heart surgery.

I approached the records office with trepidation. I wasn't sure what to say or even how to say it. "Hello…I need some help with a record. My name is Kristyn Huige and somehow or other, I have been declared dead; at least the banks in charge of my finances think I'm dead. Can you help me? Do you have a record of me dying at this hospital?"

"Wow…you don't look very dead to me. I'm sorry; I know this is not a joking matter. Can you give me the date you were released from the hospital, your insurance card and your identification card?"

I presented the clerk with the information she requested and she embarked on a search of her records. I wondered how this mess could happen. I thought that fixing this problem would be easy…should be easy. You would think that the only thing I would need to do would be present my identification and say, "I'm alive." Apparently, it's easier to declare someone dead than to decide that she's alive. Finally, the clerk came back to her desk.

"I had some trouble finding your record, but I finally did locate it. No death certificate was issued, according to the file. I can't give you any information that will help you get your identity back. All that you need to do is to prove to the bank that you're alive."

Apparently, the credit reporting agencies also had a record of my death, and my conversation with one of them did not help me clarify what I needed to do. Again, I was told I would need to prove I was alive. My question again was, "HOW?"

Since I couldn't think of anything other than showing my identification, passport and driver's license, I decided to return to the bank.

The bank manager greeted me. "Any luck yet?"

"No, but the hospital has no record of a death certificate being issued in my name. Does that help?"

It seemed bizarre to me that here we were, two adults, carrying on a conversation about whether one of the duo was dead. The fact that we were talking to one another should be proof enough that both of us were alive. I still did not have proof that I was who I said I was. I decided that this was so crazy that the only solution was to enter into the craziness.

I told the manager, "I'm not leaving here until you reinstate my cards and my accounts. You needed a death certificate to close these accounts legally. You do not have one. I think the ID I've presented here should prove who I am. Someone made a mistake and I'm the one who is suffering because of it. Call for help if you need it. Maybe someone in your company can unravel my problem. My problem apparently began here and I'm not leaving until it is settled here."

The day dragged on, with the manager and his clerks checking in on me frequently. I did add, however, that perhaps the news media would be interested in this bank having a problem as serious as this one and there seemed no solution forthcoming. This statement did seem to increase the fervor with which my problem was considered. I saw people make a lot of phone calls, and finally, the manager said he would allow me to use one card while they investigated my problem. I was surprised that an investigation was not already underway. I was not declared alive, but I had some money available to me. I guess my resurrection would come later. I was restored to "living status" in the space of a week or so. I still have no idea as to how I proved I was alive.

This whole episode really shook me up. I had been so sick and had survived. The issue of life and death was seldom far from my thoughts. It was almost as though the financial institutions in my life had made the decision for me. I felt frightened. I had "kind of" won against the bank, but my body felt the pain and anguish I imagined accompanying a near-death experience. It was almost as though what I had feared the most had actually happened. I thought that perhaps life and death are not so far apart. I felt I had lived with death for several days, and I was definitely ready to be free from constantly thinking about it.

RETURN TO EL SALVADOR 2015

"Mom, I just got this strange email. It's from someone who says they're from El Salvador…from the government. They want me to come and visit. They even say they will pay all the expenses."

"Oh, honey, it's probably just a spam email. Don't pay attention to it. Just discard it."

Sara looked confused and not quite ready to push the button that would eliminate this possible experience from her life. She hadn't thought about El Salvador for years. She was now a mother with four children and she had a very busy life. She had responsibilities and couldn't possibly desert them for a week or so. The email was probably spam, just as Mom said.

The phone rang and Kurdt was on the line. "Hi, Mom, guess what? I just got an email from the Salvadoran government…at least, that's who they said they were. They're offering me a trip to El Salvador, all expenses paid, and they will connect me to my family members who live there. Can you imagine that? They said they will do a DNA analysis of my blood so they can be sure that they connect the correct family with the right person."

I responded: "Sara got the same email just a short while ago. We're not sure if it is spam, but it sure sounds like it. Are they asking for any money from you? What do they want? If you go there, what will they want from you? Any idea as to what our State Department might say about this?"

"You have a lot of good questions, Mom, but I have to admit that I am interested. I haven't thought about El Salvador for a long time, but now that I'm reminded, I do wonder whether or not my grandmother is still alive, and there are uncles and aunts and other family members. But I still wonder why they didn't take us in when Mom was killed. We were taken to the orphanage and it wasn't that far away. I don't like thinking about what life was like when I lived there. I don't know if I want to bring the past back. I think I'm going to check this out. It might be legitimate. You never know. Do you know what Sara wants to do? Is she interested in going?"

"I don't know, but I'll have her call you. I think she might have too much on her plate to think about going now. I still don't think it is real. Why would a country invite people back to visit and pay all the expenses for this visit? Check with the State Department and see what they have to say."

I couldn't believe the multitude of feelings I had at the thought of my children going back to the country that held the trauma of their childhoods. Life in El Salvador had been horrible for them, and no one had been there when they needed comforting. Thirty-five years had passed since they had lived in El Salvador. They had dealt with nightmares and pain. There were no pleasant memories of carefree childhoods. Why now?

What was I afraid of? I thought of my own desire to go back to the place and time of my childhood where I had felt cared for and understood. When I did return to Belgium, it was not a good experience. Everything had changed and I was not prepared for that. Neither of my children had expressed any desire to return to their birth country. That's not quite true; as I remember events, Kurdt had said he wanted to go to El Salvador at a time when he was furious with me and he thought this statement would hurt my feelings. It was on the day that the judge was finalizing the adoption. The social worker had made it clear to Kurdt that the correct answer when the judge asked if he wanted to be adopted was, "Yes, I do." Suddenly I was feeling somewhat shaky in my relationship with my children. Would they choose El Salvador over me? Would their Salvadoran family suddenly be more important to them than the family we had built together? Would I lose them if they took this trip? I had to remind myself that this was not about me.

We investigated, and discovered that this was a legitimate invitation from the country of El Salvador. They were trying to connect families with the children they had lost during the worst of the violent years of internal warfare. They would do a DNA analysis so that they would be dealing with blood relatives and would not mistakenly connect the wrong people. Kurdt decided to take this trip. Sara was not ready to go. She felt fearful and didn't really remember any family members. Rosa, Kurdt's step-sister, decided to go with Kurdt.

The Salvadoran government paid for the airfare and a very nice hotel for a week. Kurdt and Rosa were provided with a protection unit everywhere they went. The government got family members together and arranged for a welcome home party where all of the family was invited. All of the food and party decorations were provided. The gathering was very emotional for Kurdt, as he remembered many of the people, especially his grandmother. Since neither Kurdt or Rosa spoke any Spanish, an interpreter had also been provided so they could at least converse with one another. They toured the area around which they had lived and visited the shack which had been their home. They also visited the orphanage. While all of this was going on, the government officials took videos and photos of the reunions. These pictures were shared with the Salvadoran people and everyone seemed pleased with the reunions.

Kurdt was surprised that there were armed guards at every corner. It was clear to him that this country was still troubled by violence. He was grateful for their protection unit as these people had taken them anywhere they wanted to go and had shown them the country. He was aware that the threat of violence was everywhere. He only felt safe because of their assigned guards.

On arriving home, Kurdt was happy to feel safe. He called me and spoke excitedly.

"Mom, I'm home. I'm so glad I went on this trip. I was terrified, but curious. I can't believe I saw my grandmother. It was wonderful to hug her. The family in Salvador are poor beyond belief. They have so little. I can't believe how they live. They have nothing. I'm so glad I live here! The agents protecting us warned us not to send money, but I think I will send them some. They did say that it was not against the law to do so. It's so hard to believe that people can be so poor. I put a lot of my issues to rest during this trip. I no longer feel abandoned by the family. I'm so happy that I went."

Sara waited a while. She had reasons for not going, but they were more like excuses. She was afraid. She didn't have the memories that Kurdt had. She only remembered bits and pieces of her life in the orphanage. Finally, about a year or so later, Sara decided to take the trip herself. She spoke with her step-brother Oscar (he had been adopted by a family in West Virginia) and the two of them went together.

Sara's experience was quite different from Kurdt's. She felt little or no connection with her mother's family. She had no memory of any of them. She was shocked when she observed the level of poverty. She saw the house she had lived in and remembered that she had seen her mother shot and killed in that home. Her experience with her mother's family was painful. What was wonderful for Sara, however, was that she was introduced to her father's family. She did not have the same father as Kurdt, and he had often told her that her father had been cruel. Her father had died a few years earlier, but she discovered that she had three step-brothers and a step-sister, and she really liked these people. They took her in and she felt accepted. They also did not seem as poor as her mother's family. They were more educated and had jobs. One brother was even building a house. The most wonderful thing that they told Sara was that their father had loved her and that he had looked for her until the day he died. Sara had always felt abandoned, and all she needed to hear was that her father missed her and looked for her. This trip put her at ease. Sara said she could put many issues away and going back to El Salvador had helped her feel grateful when it came to her life now. She appreciated our relationship more than ever.

I'm happy that I did not stand in the way of my kids going back to their homeland. I was fearful that I might lose them, but I did not try to talk them out of going. I kept my mouth shut. It was not easy staying quiet. I did not want to taint their journey in any way. Kurdt and Sara were both grateful that the Salvadoran government provided this trip for them. They were able to fill in gaps in their memories and remember some of the good people who had been part of their young lives. I am grateful that our family relationships are solid. We belong together and really appreciate one another.

Kurdt and his Salvadoran grandmother 5-9-2014

LIFE GOES ON 2016-2017

Recovering from major heart surgery took a very long time. I was obsessed with a fear of dying. Surgery and having been declared dead did not help my recovery. I wanted to live. I had never wanted to live more than I did at this point in my life. I had so much to live for. I was fortunate that I had four young people to look after me and I was grateful that I could still look after them. They brought so much joy to my life that I had no reason to complain. Every day seemed filled with new ideas, new projects, and laughter. I enjoyed my children and my grandchildren. Adopting my children was the very best thing I have ever done. I can't imagine my life without them.

My home was still full, as was my life. Sara's children and Kurdt's children were all going to school, working and enjoying family life. There were still concerts to attend, orchestra, band and choir. The time when you had to hold your ears to survive concert night was over, and the music was actually wonderful. It was a struggle for me to walk from the parking lot to the theater or music hall, but I managed to make it each time. I feel myself getting older, and it seems to take longer to recover from major and minor issues. I'm really aware of time passing when I see the growth in my grandchildren. They are all getting closer to the time when they will leave the nest.

There is a bird's nest outside my bedroom window and I've watched families of birds use this nest for the past several years. I've watched parent birds bring new twigs and straw to fortify the old nest. They do careful renovations and upkeep on their chosen home.

When the eggs appear in the nest, I've watched them meticulously cared for by parents who continue to hover as the chicks are born. Feeding the babies is an all-day project, but the parents never seem to tire of their tasks. And then…finally…departure time. I watched for many hours and wrote a poem.

THE NEST

IT'S GONE

MUD, STICKS, FEATHERS

DELICATE TAPESTRY

MULTI-YEAR HOME FOR EGGS/HATCHLINGS

FOR NOISY, HUNGRY, OPEN MOUTHS

FOR ANXIOUS PARENTS

WATCHING NEW FLIGHT.

IT'S GONE

TAKEN BY THE WIND!

CHILDREN WATCHING SCENES

OF BIRTH, OF GROWTH

OF TAKING TO AIR

FLIGHT TO NEW ADVENTURES

ABANDONING NESTS

LEAVING HOME

NEW WORLDS BECKON

FACING CHANGED LIVES

PARENTS LOOK ON

AMAZED AT TRANSFORMATION

HAPPY AND SAD

A NEW DAY FOR ALL

I'm thinking about our young ones preparing to take flight. They seem so independent. I don't remember actually feeling ready to be on my own. But I did go on my own. It was hard for me, a struggle, but I did it. It appears that all of my grandkids are eager for independence and are ready to take on everything that this entails. I think, if we're lucky, we'll be able to keep them home for a few more years. I know that Sara's children will be off to university as soon as high school is over. For Anthony, that's happening now. Alex has been working full-time in a recycling plant. The others are still in school…from preschool to grade twelve. All are busy…and in a healthy way.

Everyone in the house is taking on greater responsibility. We are all sharing cooking and cleaning and believe it or not, Anthony and Matthew are doing most of the grocery shopping. They are much more restrained when it comes to buying as they work from a menu and a carefully crafted grocery list. I don't believe I have ever been this organized, but I am learning. You're never too old to learn new tricks…I'm told. It is hard for me to give up some of the tasks I believe I'm skilled at. It's almost as though I'm losing something, some part of me is going missing. I love doing things, and taking care of all of them. I feel a special warmth with the giving. I don't want to lose any of this. But it is wonderful seeing the young take charge and move on. I just don't like it when they actually take flight and move out. I miss them so much.

A BUMP IN THE ROAD…A BIG BUMP

Life had been moving along beautifully…no hitches in the road…and then a phone call…"Sara, it's me, Gerry, I need you…I had an accident…I'm dizzy. I need you." It was March 2019. The family had not heard from Gerry for a while. He had never been good at remembering birthdays or holidays. He would come to the house when invited but never initiated anything himself. For the kids, he was an absent father, and they chose not to seek him out. Suddenly, here he was, in trouble. Sara went to see him at the hospital. He had suffered a massive stroke.

Gerry's stroke was not immediately diagnosed. For some reason that I don't fully understand, he spent about a week at the University Hospital and then was transferred to St. Joe's, where they finally did some images of his head and discovered a serious bleed. Because his problem was not dealt with immediately, he has many residual deficits. He has difficulty walking and communicating, but he can do both with assistance. He has had a considerable amount of rehabilitation but does not put much energy into getting better. He cannot return to his job as an engineer.

Sara and Gerry have been separated since 2004, but neither has chosen to divorce. They separated because he abused the boys and Sara and because of his hoarding behavior. One might say that their relationship is very complicated. Sara and the kids feel mainly frustrated and angry as they think that he is responsible for his physical problems because he has not taken the medications he needs, he is eating a diet of junk food and he is ignoring his diabetes.

I was sad that this happened, but I was also thinking about whether this was going to be another person I needed to take care of…someone I was not fond of. I did not want to take care of him. Shades of my father. What did I fail to learn from that experience? Maybe that's why I'm revisiting the feelings I had when my father died. I felt for Sara as she was technically responsible for him.

The kids and Sara called Gerry's mother and insisted that someone from his biological family come to Ann Arbor and take part in planning for Gerry. His family had not acknowledged that Sara and the kids even existed. For years, Gerry's parents and sisters had refused to be a part of the children's lives. I hoped that some of the differences could be put aside by this meeting concerning Gerry's future. The meeting was horrible. They wanted no responsibility for Gerry and accused the children of being mean to their father. They said it was up to the children to take care of Gerry and it did not matter that he had been abusive. They yelled at the kids and called them selfish and ungrateful, adding to the trauma the kids were already trying to deal with. Someone had to agree to be in charge of Gerry's care. The room was silent, and the doctors looked at Sara and me. Neither one of us had the heart to say that Gerry was on his own. We accepted responsibility. We found a nursing home for him and the boys have continued looking after his finances. His family of origin has done nothing to help us.

As of the Spring of 2019, his diabetes is generally out of control. He has terrible sores on his legs and feet and he picks at them at every opportunity, leaving them bloody and open to infection. He has similar sores on his arms. In many ways, he is pathetic and I feel sorry for him; however, I know that I will not care for him in my home.

While the family was dealing with Gerry and hospitals, Sara was behaving strangely at times. I thought the stress was getting to her. She had behaved inappropriately in the movies, at a school function and in Gerry's nursing home. I chalked it up to Sara being Sara…she had always been a bit unusual in her behavior. The kids would confront her, but she would say she was only joking. I always thought that it was Sara's attempt to be the center of attention. Her present behavior was, however, increasingly more provocative.

SARA'S BIG BUMP! WHAT IS GOING ON?

It was late April 2019. The weather was sunny and very mild. I was taking a much-needed relaxing walk outside. Feeling free. Gerry was in a placement where he was taken care of and we didn't have to spend time with him. We could all, once more, breathe deeply, and go on with our lives. The stress we were feeling was diminishing. The kids were enjoying school and their various activities. My work as a Realtor was keeping me busy. All seemed great in our world.

One day, Sara came to us at dinner and announced: "I'm leaving. I want to go and see the butterflies in New Mexico. I'm giving up custody of the girls."

We were all shocked. The air felt charged. The silence was deafening. No one could think of anything to say. The girls started to cry and ran to their rooms. Relationships with Sara had been strained as we tended not to see eye to eye on most issues. However, I was completely taken by surprise. This made no sense to me at all. "Where did this idea come from? What was going on? Oh my God…!

Anthony spoke up first: "When do you plan on doing this? Do you plan on coming back?"

Sara casually responded: "I don't intend to come back. I'll probably leave soon. I'm not entirely sure. I'll leave before school lets out."

I said, "You need to give us time to go to a lawyer and get custody set up." I was furious and trying hard not to lose my cool. I couldn't believe she was actually planning to abandon her family….her children…me. "Can we at least talk about this?"

"Yeah, but it won't change anything."

"Why won't it change anything? This is such a big move…think of what you're doing to the kids."

Everybody was shouting at this point but Sara wasn't even pretending to listen. She seemed relaxed and I could almost say…happy. The entire scene felt like something from a very bad movie. I could not believe what was going on. She wants to abandon the family!

"Are you really serious about this plan? Do you even have a plan? Is this a bad joke? Is this another of your provocations?" I asked.

Sara kept her head down and ignored my questions. The kids left the room in various states of rage, anxiety, depression and fear. I left the kitchen in shock, but I was ready to get our lawyer on the phone to see what I needed to do to get custody of the girls. Anthony, Matthew and I spent some time trying to get a grip on this situation. When I think about this scenario years later, anger stands out as the predominant emotion the boys and I felt. The girls were both angry and afraid. We were all furious with Sara, the girls included. I think we were all ready to kick her out of the house. We were fed up with her antics.

Later in the day, we all decided that if Sara wanted to leave, she could leave, but she needed to give us the time to arrange custody. We told her, "Leave if that is what you want, but if you won't tell us that you're coming back…then don't come back. We don't want to sit around wondering whether or not you will return."

I'm sure that I have only a minimal idea of what the kids were going through. First, they had all of that turmoil with Gerry and his family. Dealing with the anger and fear during and after that event was very difficult. They were no longer kids when it came to carefree adolescent experiences. They were responsible for their father, making medical and financial decisions for him, while feeling an intense desire to separate themselves from him. Now…their mother wants to abandon them. All of this was happening within one month's time. I reminded myself of their ages: 15,17,19,21. They were too young for all of this.

It was the last day of school, and Sara had said she would leave by that day. She was lying on her bed with all of her possessions around her and she didn't look like she was going to move any time in the near future. Matthew and Natalie were trying to move her along, but she was not moving.

"You have to go, Sara. You said you were leaving today. You can't just play with our feelings," I shouted.

"I'm not ready yet; give me some time…don't rush me!" Sara whined.

Matthew joined us and urged her on with, "I'll help you pack and take your stuff out."

We were fed up with the way Sara had behaved for the last several months. SHE said SHE wanted to leave and we were ready to see her go. As Sara delayed and delayed this departure, I began to wonder what was going on with her. Was she sick?

"Are you sick and do you want me to take you to the emergency room?"

"No, I'm fine," Sara said as she waved me away. "Go away!" She added.

Sara continued having trouble putting her possessions in the car. Matthew pitched in, as did Natalie and finally, around 6 pm, the car was loaded and she was ready to take off.

As we watched the Ford Escape pull out of the driveway, I felt drained of all of my feelings and energy. I looked at the kids and they were all in a terrible state. Everyone looked ashen, their faces immobile. All were silent, in shock. We walked back into the house. No one spoke. We stood in silence in the kitchen for a short time. Slowly, we all turned and went to our respective bedrooms. I went to my room and cried. I felt like a mean person. I was so worried about Sara. I really felt that there was something going on I was not seeing. How could this happen to these kids? First their Dad and now their Mom. We need to keep talking about what is happening. Dealing with this kind of abandonment is not easy.

We got occasional texts from Sara, but they made little or no sense. We were worried. I told myself that I should have insisted that we go to the hospital to check her out. I thought that she might be having an emotional breakdown. We decided that no one should be given a hard time for what we did in "kicking Sara out." The kids were able to track her using the GPS on her phone and she did make it to New Mexico. We prayed that she was okay.

One evening, we got a phone call from a small hospital in New Mexico. A doctor asked if we knew someone named Sara. Eagerly, we shouted, "Yes."

"We are treating a young woman who was brought to us by the state police. She'd been wandering in the desert and was unable to talk. She doesn't know where she is or where she should be. We found some identification. Are you her family?"

"Yes, we are. What is going on with her? How is she?"Anthony responded.

"We have diagnosed her with small cell lung cancer which has metastasized to her brain. You need to come immediately. She is being transferred to the University Hospital in Albuquerque and will probably need immediate surgery. Her condition is critical."

Once more, we were all in shock. We got the information we needed from the doctor and then began to talk to each other. This was why she had been acting so strangely the last year or so. Our feelings were all over the place. I felt both fear and anger. While I was glad to finally know what was wrong, another part of me had actually enjoyed life at home without Sara. Everything seemed much less complicated. The kids were doing what they needed to do. They had always gotten along with each other and were once more enjoying each other's company. They seldom argued. We had told her she couldn't come back and now she was coming back. I have to admit that I was glad she would be back with us. As hard as she was to live with at times, I loved her. Would things again be contentious? But…first things first…I had to go to New Mexico.

To get to New Mexico, I had to make a stop in Atlanta. This was great, as Corrie offered to fly with me from Atlanta to Albuquerque. We got there, rented a car, and were quickly off to the University Hospital. The doctor met us there and told us her condition was grave. When we saw her, she did not initially know Corrie and me. It was hard to recognize her as her long, dark hair was incredibly wild and her face was swollen. It was as if she had not washed or combed her hair in weeks. She had major trouble speaking and finding words. I couldn't believe her condition. It took a few hours for her to finally realize who I was. She clutched my hand and wouldn't let me go. She was terrified. I tried to reassure her…told her where she was…told her that she was very sick but that the doctor would help her. I told her that Corrie and I would be there for her. The doctor told us her surgery would be tomorrow afternoon.

"Sara, do you know where your car is? We need to find it." I asked quietly.

"McDonald's," she said shakily.

Corrie and I looked at each other. Sara had been picked up about one hundred miles east of Albuquerque. She frequently texted about McDonald's. Now we had to find a McDonald's. We asked the police about where she was found and if there was a McDonald's nearby. We started out driving and headed east. About one hundred miles later, we got lucky. We saw a McDonald's and a red Escape. Her car was parked at a McDonald's! We found the place and the car. I find myself repeating myself as I am still astonished that we found the car so easily. The McDonald's people had been keeping an eye on the car and proved to be very helpful. The car was a total mess. I couldn't believe how badly it smelled. Sara had apparently lost control of her bowels as her illness became more acute and for the last several weeks, had lived in the car which was full of excrement. Corrie and I held our noses and tried to figure out what to toss in the garbage. McDonald's said we could use their dumpster and gave us towels and disinfectant spray. We tossed more and more of her stuff that was destroyed. It was probably 115 degrees F and we were fading fast, when I got a call from the hospital that Sara's surgery was moved up and we needed to get there immediately.

I won the toss as to who would drive the car to the storage place. I felt sick from the smell, from the heat and from the horrible circumstances. For some reason, I was emotionally moved by the process of tossing most of Sara's possessions. I couldn't believe how sad I felt. These were my daughter's things that I was throwing away. We were at a loss as to what else we could do, so we tossed all that we could, and left the rest of the stuff in the car. I drove that intolerably smelly car back to Albuquerque with all of the windows open and the hot air baking me. Corrie was the lucky one and could drive the rental. We found the long-term lot on the way to the hospital and left the smelly Ford there until someone would return to drive it back to Michigan. I needed to park my feelings for the time being in order to deal with what was really important.

We saw Sara before the surgery and she was not doing well. The doctor said he was going to try to remove the large tumor on her frontal lobe and several tumors below it. She had a number of tumors on her brain stem and others in various locations all over her brain. I was terrified for her. For the first time, I was coming to grips with the possibility of losing her, and all I could say was, "I'm not ready for that." Sara was only forty-three years old and too young to die. She had been with me since she was five years old.

The last two days had completely turned our lives upside down. I was not ready to lose my child. She had much more living to do and I was aware that her kids were not prepared to let her go.

Sara survived the operation, but the doctors were only able to make the frontal lobe tumor smaller; it was too vascular to remove. They were unable to do anything with the other tumors they had planned to remove. The doctors said that not much could be done for Sara and that she would not live long…several months was their guess. She remained in the ICU for four more days and then she was transferred to a rehabilitation hospital. She was like a small child, confused about who she was and where she was. She was not confused about who I was. I told her that Corrie and I needed to go back home so that I could arrange to bring her home. I don't think she understood me, but she said "okay". It was August 2019. I left New Mexico in shock and in tears.

It was wonderful having Corrie with me at this terrible time. She was incredibly competent and supportive. We spoke of many of our concerns. Her nursing background was very helpful in giving me ideas as to what we would be dealing with. We spoke about death and final days. We spoke about our own fears when it came to illness, incapacity, and death. She helped me sort out what I would be able to do for Sara and what I would need to get help with. She told me that this was more than a one-person job, and that the kids and I needed to work together. She also encouraged me to seek out community help, such as Hospice. Just hearing the name "Hospice" raised my anxiety level and brought on tears. Corrie reassured me that she would be there for me. I really love and appreciate her.

Once home, I needed to deal with the kids. How do children, young adults, deal with the loss of both parents? They were angry, hurt, and frustrated. They felt this way when Sara gave up custody of the girls. I pointed out that the cancer, particularly the brain cancer on her frontal lobe, was probably the main reason for her erratic behavior, and that she had probably not been in condition to make any rational decisions for the past year. I hoped that this would help them feel that the "real" Sara didn't abandon them but that the malfunctioning of her brain had produced the poor decisions she had made lately. They understood what I was saying, but it would take time for anything to assuage their feelings of abandonment. To be honest, we were all worried and angry. I told them to give themselves time to absorb all of what was happening. I didn't expect that they would instantly forgive Sara on hearing of her brain's involvement with her behavior. We needed time.

I was convinced that we would make it through this stressful time. We are all survivors, and we will do what needs to be done. I felt myself gear up for another battle. No matter what happens, we will bring Sara back and resolve our issues with her. I knew we were in for a difficult time.

A PAINFUL HOMECOMING

The children and I had to find a way of getting Sara home. When she would be ready to fly, would I be able to manage her on the plane? Would she be able to walk? Perhaps I could get her on an Angel flight, as the medics on board this kind of flight could handle her medical issues. Would she be in a condition to fly a commercial airline? I had so many questions and no answers yet. Everything depended on Sara's condition in a few weeks.

I found out that Angel flights were very expensive, well over $20,000.00, and I knew we did not have the money for this kind of flight. There were free angel flights, but they had a maximum distance of nine hundred miles, and this was about twice this distance. We started a "go fund me" page and managed to get some funds, but not nearly enough for an angel flight. I was amazed and deeply touched by people's generosity and prayers. Everyone wanted to help. Neighbors, people from church and scouting families provided meals and emotional support.

We were finally told that Sara was ready to come home after about three weeks, and we decided that all we could do was a commercial flight. We ruled out coming back in the Ford Escape since that would take at least 3 days and I knew I couldn't handle going in and out of the car with Sara, and we weren't sure if it would be tolerable due to the smell. So…a commercial airline with one-stop was our only choice…here we go. We had no idea what we were getting into.

I knew that I could not bring Sara home by myself, so I was happy when a neighbor, Wally, agreed to come with me and help me with this task. I told the airline about our situation, and they said they would have a wheelchair available and that they would help us. We didn't realize at the time that we would need much more help than a wheelchair. So…off we went. When we saw Sara at the rehabilitation facility, she was doing better. It was clear to me that she had a very long way to go. I felt uncertain that she was in a condition to travel. I asked questions… "Can she stand up…can she switch chairs? Can she travel?" We were told she could stand and switch chairs with help. We had no idea how much help. Her speech was very limited, and I was uncertain as to what she really understood when I told her we were going to take her home. She thought the facility she was in was her home and she was reluctant to leave. She was very confused as to what "home" meant. When I watched the staff get her ready to travel, she didn't seem able to understand their directions so that she could help in the process. I was concerned. Sara had gained a good deal of weight and at 5 feet 1 inch, she weighed around 230 pounds. If we needed to lift her, I knew I could not do it, and I was pretty sure that Wally could not either.

Our first problem occurred at the airport when we were trying to get her into a wheelchair. We had been told she could stand and assist us, but she clearly could not. We were trying to lift her into the chair and she fell and injured her leg. She howled like a small child in pain. We thought she would be able to stand, pivot, and even take a step. Even with our help, she was not able to stand. My neighbor and I were both elderly, and neither of us had the strength to pick her up. Finally, I begged the airline personnel and they came out and helped us get her in the wheelchair. Unfortunately, she needed to go to the bathroom, so we were once more struggling to help her, and again, the people from the airline helped after more begging. She needed two skilled young people to help her. We had clearly been misinformed as to her readiness to fly on a commercial plane. At this point, I was worried that the airline would decide that she was too handicapped to travel on this commercial flight. Sara kept looking at my face and I knew that all she saw was anger and frustration…and she was correct. I didn't want to scare her, but I couldn't change the expression on my face.

She kept saying, "Mom mad?... Mom mad?

"I'm not mad at you, Sara," I said, hoping I didn't sound how I felt. "I'm just upset that everything seems so hard to do. But I'm not mad at you." But, in truth, I was angry with her.

When we finally got to the gate, she again had to be moved to a chair that could go down the aisle of an airliner. We were grateful that the professionals moved her on and off the plane. We had to change planes in Denver, as there are no direct flights between Detroit and Albuquerque. If things were not already bad…they got much worse. Luck would have it…the plane was assigned the gate at the farthest end of the airport…and…we had to exit the plane onto the tarmac. This meant that the crew had to carry Sara in her chair down a long stairway to the tarmac and then up a stairway to the gate. The crew, of course, decided that Sara would be the last person off the plane, and then they debated who would carry her and the wheelchair.

My neighbor and I were in a panic, waiting for all of the above to happen, as we had a limited amount of time before our connecting flight was scheduled to take off. The whole ordeal of getting Sara off the plane and into the airport took forty-five minutes. The airline crew closed the blinds so that we could not see or take pictures of what was happening with Sara and her chair, but they finally appeared at the gate and we had several minutes to run a mile for the next flight. Since my heart surgery, I have not run, but at this moment…I did the best run that I could. When we got to our gate, the doors had just closed, but they opened them for us. I can't believe how much I prayed and how thankful I was. I could barely breathe. My chest hurt, my legs hurt, and I was fearful that I would have a heart attack. If I had to run any further, I could not have done so. Sara looked like she had enjoyed the entire run through the airport.

"Weee! Weee!" she exclaimed as the attendant ran with her in the chair.

If it had not been clear to me before, it was now clear to me that I would not be able to look after Sara at home when we finally got home. If I were to survive this episode in our family's life experience, I would need a new plan.

Sara appeared increasingly confused as the flight continued. I felt so guilty at the thought of not taking her home. I tried to address the issue with Sara, but she did not understand. While flying from Denver to Detroit, I gathered my thoughts about what I would do. For the past several weeks, I had spoken to the people at the Rogel Cancer Center at the University of Michigan hospital, and had sent Sara's records. I had wanted them to evaluate her and follow her medically. They agreed, but I did not realize that I could not care for her at home in her present condition. I knew that we did not have the supplies or equipment to deal with someone who needed help at the level that Sara clearly needed assistance. She needed help with all of her personal care: diapers, bath, standing, moving from bed to a chair, and she needed a hospital bed. I was not prepared for any of this. I knew I did not have the personal or physical strength to take care of all of these needs. If she were admitted to the hospital, I would have some time to prepare for the reality of her condition.

Our friend Sue picked us up at the airport, and we decided to take Wally home and then we would take Sara directly to the University Hospital. We went directly to the Emergency Room. The staff did not really understand why I had brought her to them. She had just been released from a rehabilitation facility and what did I want them to do? I wanted them to admit her for evaluation. We waited for hours. Sara slept on and off, but I was not budging on my decision that she needed to be in the hospital and had to be evaluated. I was finally able to speak to a social worker who understood what I was saying. She understood that I could not look after her at home and that we needed a full evaluation. The staff had no idea what to do in these circumstances. Thank God that the social worker understood what I was saying. Sara was admitted.

Sara was exhausted and very confused. She didn't understand that she was not going home. She wanted to go home. We were at Emergency most of the night, and Sara slept on and off. The Hospital finally decided to admit her. She spent two weeks in the hospital and then three weeks in a Rehabilitation Hospital. In the meantime, she had a full evaluation and had also begun radiation therapy. She was due to start chemotherapy if her insurance would cover the incredible cost of $17,000.00 per month. The insurance agreed to pay for her treatment. It was hoped that this drug would extend her life. The doctor was clear that this was not a cure.

Once on the chemotherapy, Sara had severe reactions to the drug. We were grateful that the drug was paid for, but the doctor said she would be on this medication until she died. Her prognosis saw her disease as terminal. In New Mexico, the medical staff had thought she had only a few months. The drug program and the radiation at Michigan had the sole purpose of extending her life. She started the drug in September and from the first day, she could not keep food or water down. She threw up constantly. I worried about dehydration and kidney problems.

Sara was wonderful. She never complained and was never demanding. Her strange, provocative behavior which had been so annoying, was gone. She was that sweet kid I had brought home from Cleveland on that wonderful Mother's Day. I felt totally helpless. I would have given anything to provide some semblance of help for her that was more than simply caring for basic needs. I didn't know what to do with my energy…I couldn't help her. All I could do was love her.

Finally, in late December, Sara became so ill that I took her to the emergency room and they admitted her again. She was terribly dehydrated and very sick. The doctors did another craniotomy and repaired some of the work done in the earlier surgery. This time, they shaved her head. I had been shocked that the New Mexico surgeons had not done so to open her skull as she had long hair which had feces in it from her time living in her car. At this time, in December 2019, she decided she did not want to continue living like this. It was not a life with any quality: staying in her bed, unable to eat, feeling sick and throwing up even the water she drank. She decided that if she did have a limited amount of time left in this world, she wanted to feel better and be able to relate to her family. She hoped to be able to eat again.

I hated the idea of Sara not continuing chemo, as I still held out hope that she could be cured. I did see her point and fully understood what she was saying. The last three months were certainly not the way anyone would want to live. She stopped therapy. The medical staff was wonderfully supportive. They hoped that she could continue on some level with chemotherapy, but Sara had enough. She was done. They honored that and agreed to just keep an eye on her and have an occasional medical check-up. She began palliative care which would become hospice care when needed.

I took Sara home from a doctor's appointment in early January 2020. We both felt relieved and very positive about the decision she had made. To be completely honest, I wasn't so sure about how I felt. On one level, I supported her decision, but I wasn't ready to give up. I couldn't accept that my child was going to die…at least not now. She seemed so ready for this new journey. Even though I understood her decision to let her body "go", I felt such a deep sadness. This was another road we had never traveled before. What would happen? What would it be like to face death? I couldn't bear to let her go, but watching her suffer the way she had was also not the answer. The doctors checked in with her several times over the next few months, but she had had no further chemo. At this point, I wondered what the status of the cancer was, and what would happen in the future. I didn't like all of the unknowns in our lives. I needed to know the path we were choosing. I wanted to know what was going to happen, but I had to accept that not knowing was part of being alive.

In April 2021, Sara was still alive. She seemed to enjoy her life. She slept quite a bit, but on the whole, was pain free. At least, this was what she reported to me when I asked. She walked with a pronounced limp and was severely hunched over, but she could walk. The kids tried to nudge her into getting involved with life. It was always too easy for me to wait on Sara, and the kids made it clear that she needed to take care of herself more than she did. She was on the dishwashing list and had to make occasional meals. I did her laundry, but she was pretty much self-sufficient when it came to her personal needs. She loved watching TV either alone or with one of us. She didn't like company in the house, but she never liked people around, so this was not new. She was quiet and, in many ways, difficult to converse with. She remained ignorant when it came to local, national or world news. She did not want visits from friends and seldom spoke with them should they drop in. If the kids needed permission for anything, they came to me or to Anthony, so Sara was out of the parenting loop. Sara has said she was happy with the world as it presented itself. She was basically waiting to die.

A LIFE

What is this?

This lump

This inert blanket covered

Bit of protoplasm

My Child!

My love!

My little girl

So vulnerable

Half in

Half out

Of this world.

Slipping away

I cannot stop the drift.

Where are you now?

Sara speaks at my intrusion.

"I'm alive."

"I haven't gone yet."

Reassurance falls on deaf ears.

She rises painfully

The TV beckons

It's just another evening

In this long farewell. (2021)

(From my diary, August 2021.) *Sara is still alive. It's been a year and a half since her decision to let nature take its course. She is able to eat anything she wants without nausea, she can minimally help in the family, and she states she enjoys life. The only symptom we notice is that her senses of hearing, taste, and smell are severely limited. We don't know what the cancer will do, but our focus is not on her illness but on her life. We are all aware of the finality of life. None of us knows when our time will be up. Making each moment count is my focus. I also look to learn something new each day.*

Sara has a different outlook and, I have to admit, that the rest of the family and I are confused and frustrated. She refuses to set any goals, even limited ones. "There is nothing I really want to do." The Make a Wish people have a program for adults. She could take a trip to any place she might want to go...with the family...and have a real family vacation. She said "no". Even though she is able to walk or could be pushed in a wheelchair, she only seems to want to watch television and move from bed to chair. She says that she is tired. She states clearly that she is not depressed. There is just nothing she wants to do. I've never experienced anyone who is so ready to let nature take its course. It's as though she's saying: "Well, I'm done."

It is ironic that when Sara was very young, she kept insisting that she would die when she was forty-six. I kept trying to convince her that she had a long life ahead of her. I showed her tables outlining how long average male and female lifetimes were, but the information was meaningless to Sara. She had her mind made up. I thought that arguing about this made no sense, so I kept quiet. I have no idea what the number means to her, but she keeps repeating the same number. Maybe this explains her peaceful acceptance of her fate. In some ways, she couldn't have chosen a better time for her long farewell. We have all been home because of Covid 19 and we have spent a good deal of time together. We spend time with Sara, encourage her, berate her, have fun watching programs with her, and nag her. We do nag her to get out of bed, to do small tasks, and to take small walks outside. Sara, however, shouts a laugh-filled "NO" and continues to enjoy the program she is watching.

She spends many hours just lying in bed, not reading, not on her phone, basically doing nothing as I interpret this behavior. To be honest, I have no idea as to what is going on in her head. She may actually be "doing something." I'm just not privy to it. I just don't understand how someone can lie awake, be alone, and be satisfied. It has become clear to me that she is not depressed; she is just choosing to be with herself. In some ways, I envy her ability to do this. I know that being alone with myself is something I have a very hard time doing. I want distractions from myself. I have even tried replicating Sara's behavior. I have lain in my bed, chosen to stay awake, only to decide after a short period of time that I can't handle this. I start to ache and I don't have pleasant conversations with myself. I'm just not comfortable with that much "me". I've asked Sara what she is thinking about…what is going on in her head? She doesn't respond.

I want Sara to embrace life, but she seems to be embracing death instead. As I think about what I have written, it's clear to me that I need to stop expecting Sara to do what I think I would do in the same circumstances. I need to accept her response to her illness. I've accepted her decision to stop treatment. I now need to let her live out the rest of her life as she sees fit. My head is filled with thoughts rushing her to "make the most of every moment you have left." I need to stop this desire to control. She wants and needs privacy, and I must give her the space she craves. It is clear to me that I am not finished with my need to know what is happening at all times...to control...to understand what is not fathomable. (personal diary August 2021)

It is now July 2024, and Sara is still with us. Needless to say, we are excited that she has not died...yet, but she sees herself as "a dying person." Her tumors are still in her brain and lung, but the chemo and radiation made them much smaller. They have maintained the smaller size for several years now. She developed a tumor on her kidney, and that was dealt with by radiation. Sara is not averse to radiation as it doesn't make her sick the way the chemo did. She receives no chemotherapy and is under palliative care. She walks the neighborhood once per day and seems to enjoy this. She tends to eat very little, but enjoys what she chooses. She has lost almost 100 pounds and is looking like her old self. I can't believe the progress she has made. She got to see all four of her children graduate from high school; two graduate from university, and one will graduate from university in December 2024. The youngest will graduate from university next spring. She was able to be a part of their growing up and participated in celebrating their accomplishments. She still spends a good deal of time in bed, playing computer games, watching television and listening to audiobooks. We do enjoy watching some shows together, and, when the kids come over, watching movies on the big screen. I am so happy that she is still alive.

COVID - 19

Kurdt and I have a wonderful relationship in many ways. We clearly love each other and share many similar traits. We both respect God and family. We are both involved in our communities and in the lives of the children we are rearing. We do have some differences, and they interfere with our communicating with one another. We are both Christian, but Kurdt and his family are Free Methodist and I am Catholic. I am happy that he believes in God and is involved in a church that will help guide him. Kurdt believes that my brand of Christianity is not valid and that I will not be "saved". His church is strongly supportive of Donald Trump and I am not. We are unable to have a civil conversation about either religion or politics. We decided not to raise these topics since we both got very upset when trying to say anything that touched on our religious or political beliefs. This ban worked for many years, and then Covid-19 struck.

The scientific truth about Covid-19 is that it is a coronavirus disease caused by SARS-CoV-2. It is very contagious and spreads like wildfire. As of June 1, 2024, nearly 1.2 million people died from this virus in the United States. You're lucky if your symptoms are mild, but this virus may attack more than your lungs and respiratory system and death can be the outcome for even young, otherwise healthy people. This insidious virus is spread by infected people breathing out microscopic particles containing the virus. If they land on your eyes, nose, mouth or hands, you might be the next victim. The spreader of the virus might even be symptom-free and not know that he's spreading death. This sounds dramatic, but it was a terrifying time for most people in their right mind. The virus was first detected in early 2020, but the public was not informed early enough for something constructive to be done about it. People were uninformed about the severity of the virus and then they were given confusing information about what they could do to protect themselves. There were wars over whether to wear a mask or not to mask. Very few masks were available for the public to use. In fact, most of the necessary medical supplies for both medical personnel and the average person, were in very short supply. It seemed common sense to me that if I agreed that the way this disease is spread in the air, then wearing a mask would help protect against getting sick. Many of us who believed that wearing a mask would help keep us somewhat safe, decided to wear masks. Others who did not agree with what the medical community advised chose not to wear a mask. If one agrees that this disease is spread in large groups of people, then confining yourself to home and family also makes sense.

Kurdt and Kelly believed that the fuss about the virus was a hoax, that all of the precautions most people were taking were unnecessary and that Covid was nothing more than a cold. They chose not to wear masks and they did not avoid large group settings. When the vaccine became available, they chose not to protect themselves and get the shot. I was willing to avoid talking about our taboo topics as long as personal welfare was not at stake. I made no headway when it came to changing their beliefs about this terrible disease. I decided to stop my attempts at rescuing them. I worried about their whole family's welfare. Kurdt believed what Mr. Trump said and that was that. Kelly had to work in health care. She had ongoing exposure and as a result, she developed a mild case of Covid. Kurdt also caught Covid. I felt angry at Kurdt and at all of the people he looked up to who spouted misinformation about this deadly disease. No matter what information I presented, I made no impact on Kurdt, so I stopped communicating about this topic. Those of us who lived together in Ann Arbor followed the suggested regimens. None of us became sick with this disease. I missed my contact with Kurdt and his family, I worried about them, and I was grateful for phones. I know of many families torn apart by conflicts of this nature. I had certainly disagreed with friends when it came to religion or politics, but the conflicts were not vicious and did not put a dagger into the heart of the relationship. We disagreed and agreed to leave the situation and get on with our friendship. The present conflicts seemed much more intense and long-lasting. I feel sad about this because we have always been able to resolve our conflicts.

As I think about this conflict, I believe that the problem we are having when it comes to communication is one related to FACTS. We do not agree with the facts of the situations we have been trying to discuss. If you don't have the same or similar ways of defining reality, then you will have a major problem even touching on differences. The conspiracies that various Trump groups espouse do not deal with truth or facts that can be proven. It's hard to debate fantasies which only seem to reside in the mind of Mr. Trump and his immediate cohort. I missed my contact with Kurdt during Covid. I missed several years of direct contact with his family.

My immediate family secluded ourselves in our home. The boys only left the home to shop for groceries, and then they wore masks and washed their hands on arriving back home. Sara and I were particularly vulnerable when it came to this disease. I needed to be watchful because of my age, and Sara because of her cancer. The kids were particularly careful in order to protect us. It was clear to me that I did not want to die and I was grateful that the others in the family also wanted me to stay alive.

Everything changed in our lives. I had been successfully working as a Realtor, and now our office was closed. Businesses were completely shut down. I had gotten used to the idea of having some money and now I was getting ready to really tighten my belt. Luckily, the federal government decided that independent agents like myself were now eligible to collect unemployment insurance. This was a first for me, and I was really happy to get this windfall. When the office opened up again, I was reluctant to go back into the realty business as covid was still a very real threat to older people in particular. I continued to collect unemployment

and slowly worked my way back into the business. While I had always done open houses when I had listings, I was now doing virtual open houses. Houses were now shown on the internet only. It was something new to learn, but I missed the direct contact with buyers.

All six of us were pretty much confined to our house, and surprisingly, we got along very well. The boys set up a movie theater in the walk-out lower level, and we enjoyed watching movies together. The kids were also involved in virtual school. All classes, high school and university, were on in-house computers only. Christina, who was a junior at Pioneer, really missed meeting with her friends. She loved social and athletic events, especially ultimate frisbee, and these were all canceled. She did not complain. Natalie had a lousy senior year as ALL of the senior activities were canceled, including graduation. She was unable to say goodbye to her friends as gatherings were limited in size and were generally discouraged. Graduation consisted of simply driving around the school parking lot, staying in the car, wearing a mask, and picking up her diploma from masked principals and teachers who cheered her on. The school did host a two-hour film retrospective for the seniors which was played on our televisions at home. Natalie was a trooper and didn't complain. She focused on university, and looked forward to starting as a freshman in engineering at the University of Michigan. When the public pools finally opened up, she spent her summer working as a lifeguard and built up her savings.

Although at-home computer classes were not as effective as in-person teaching, the kids all managed to make it work for them. The boys helped the girls when math issues came up, and everyone worked hard at their studies. When Christina was ready to graduate from high school, the school announced that the ceremony would be similar to a "regular" graduation. It would be held in the open at the school's football field and everyone would hear their names read and receive their diplomas.

What surprised me the most was that in spite of the massive amount of togetherness we were experiencing, we seemed to be enjoying being together. We ate our meals around the kitchen table and spent our time talking when we were finished. No one seemed in a hurry. We actually took time to be with one another and found ourselves laughing and enjoying our confinement. The kids were best friends before Covid, and the years spent cooped up together in our home solidified their deep love for one another.

Even though we knew that travel was dangerous when it came to Covid, we also knew that it was important for the girls to experience a college tour. I had taken Anthony when he was evaluating universities, and now Anthony took charge of this parental task. Early in the pandemic, when all of the restrictions were not yet in place, Anthony took both girls on a college tour. They started out in St. Catherines, Ontario, and spent an evening with their cousins and their grown kids. Although it was a masked visit and a lot of care had to be taken, they really enjoyed getting to know this part of the family better. Then…off to the purpose of the trip…colleges. They went to New England, New York, and Pennsylvania. They had a great time exploring the food, especially the lobster in Boston. They visited Boston College, MIT, and several other schools before moving on to Pennsylvania. Christina liked the Pittsburgh campus. They were gone for five days. Anthony paid the entire tab for this trip. Sharing what you have is definitely what I had hoped to instill in the kids, and I can see this trait in everything that they do. They had a wonderful time together and have repeated journeys like this one in other parts of the world.

Well…where did the girls decide to go to university? They both chose the University of Michigan, just like the boys. A lot went into their choice…cost, quality of education, proximity to home, and covid. So now all four of the kids will be University of Michigan grads. When the boys went to university, they chose to live at home as we live fairly close to the school and are on a bus system. Natalie decided to live in the dorms, in spite of the virus. This decision proved difficult as students were confined to their rooms and all classes were again virtual. She still enjoyed her freedom from home regardless of the limitations. She was grateful that she got to have dinners with friends. At Thanksgiving she was forced to exit the dorms as they were closed due to massive outbreaks of the virus. Natalie decided to rent an apartment with friends. She was still confined to her apartment and classes were virtual. This was not the university experience she was looking forward to. I can't help but think that renting a place under the present conditions was a waste of money. Natalie wanted to be involved in campus life and living on campus is part of that experience for her. Even though this version of campus life was not what she had hoped for, she enjoyed herself.

Matthew seemed to take everything in stride. He finally had a room of his own since we did a re-shuffling when Natalie moved to the dorms. He turned his room into a palace and he enjoyed his time in his personal space. All of his classes were virtual and he plugged away at them. April 2021 was graduation and then he looked for a job…probably out of town. He took some time off and then landed a job with Amazon as an engineer. This meant a move away from home, and he found a lovely apartment in Royal Oak. He is quite a cook and enjoys making Korean and Mexican foods. He is quiet and, like his Mom, enjoys the quiet. I tend to find it awkward talking to Matthew, except when we are in the car, and then we can talk about anything. Matthew is gentle and kind, and he clearly loves the family. He had a difficult time in middle school when he felt an enormous amount of anger at his father for his neglectful and abusive behavior. In spite of the past, he is helpful in looking after his father and does so willingly.

Anthony has taken over as the leader of the family. He handles the finances for his Mom and Dad as well as his own. He guides the girls with their budgets. Although he was working full time as an engineer, he lived at home and sheltered with Sara and myself during Covid. There was very little for us to do during our confinement with Covid. We created the menus and the boys did the shopping. I felt a bit disgruntled as I had always loved going grocery shopping. I always managed to run into friends and I enjoyed the social time. Now, it wasn't safe for me to go to stores. I really missed this time sorting through products and chatting with friends, but I knew that times had changed and I had to adapt. I couldn't wait until I was again free to wander the stores.

I needed to get used to a larder that was not stuffed full of everything under the sun…much of which would not get used. I've always had something of a starvation mentality. This is probably a remnant of living through World War II, when we did not have enough food. I'd never thought of this as a problem, but the kids were concerned about the amount of food I wasted and the cost of this waste. When I did the shopping, it was easy to pick up foods that I might use "someday." I had every excuse in the book when it came to buying food. (I might like it, I do like it, I'd like to try it, it's in a pretty box, Someone told me this is great, etc.) I didn't really think of it as an issue I needed to deal with. Well…with the boys doing the shopping…guess what happened? We started having empty shelves and a part of me began to panic. The boys reminded me that we had a plethora of grocery stores around the house. If we needed anything, they said, "We'll go and get it for you."

I insisted that "it's so nice to have everything we might need right here in the house."

Anthony said, "Grandma, take a look at the expiration dates of some of this food…some of them have been expired for five years or more…you can't eat them. Why buy things you're not going to use?"

"But I'll use them someday…maybe!"

The discussion continued and finally, I began to understand what they were saying. I felt some panic in my stomach, but I would try things their way. I would deal with the empty shelves and perhaps even learn to appreciate them…at least, that's what the girls suggested. I think it will take some time for me to feel comfortable with spaces on shelves and room in the refrigerator.

I am grateful for all of the initiative the kids have taken. They knew what they needed to do and did it without grumbling. They took the necessary precautions to protect themselves and others when going out into the world. They didn't complain; they just did what they needed to do. I really appreciated them.

To fill the time, we played cards, games, watched television, talked, and began to look around the house and found projects that needed to be done. Anthony thought we should remodel two of our bathrooms. What a wonderful idea. As I thought about this project, I wondered how we would do…a family of six…with one bathroom available. I remembered that when I was growing up, we were a family of five with one small bathroom….we made it…even when my father did not cooperate.

Anthony took charge of the renovation. We first ordered everything we would need for both bathrooms and used our garage to store everything. When we were ready, Benny, my friend and contractor, demolished and trashed everything in both bathrooms. Then the beautiful tile was installed and I no longer recognized these rooms. Within two weeks, most of the work was done and new cabinets and fixtures were installed. I discovered that Anthony had fantastic taste and I had to admit to myself that the rooms looked much better than what I had designed. I learned a lot about myself and my family. The bathrooms are actually incredibly gorgeous. I can't believe how beautiful and functional they are. Thanks, kids.

Another activity I began during our Covid time was writing. The kids and I spent time going through all of our photo albums. We ran into the pictures of the family in Europe: Dad's sixteen brothers and sisters, great, great grandparents, my Mom's family, and photos taken during the war when I was young. They were curious and wanted to know about all of these strangers, so I started telling them about who these people were. We spent some wonderful times sharing stories of the past. I discovered that my grandchildren knew nothing about my experience during World War II and my struggles after the war. As I shared my story with them, I thought others might appreciate what I had to say. I decided to write a memoir, and joined a group set up by the University of Michigan for older adults. I stayed with this group for one year, and then joined a small group when we could finally meet in person. Our group of four meets weekly for three hours, and we make very good use of our time. So far, I have written one book, *Escaping a Well of Fear,* and I am almost finished with my next book, *Journey to Family.*

2023-2024

These have been wonderful years. The boys are both working as engineers, Matthew in Detroit and Anthony in California. I miss them, but I know how important it is to venture out alone. I miss their energy when they tackle projects, their laughter when talking amongst themselves and simply their presence. The girls are also absent from the house as they are living with friends on campus. They are nearby, however, and drop in frequently. I love to hear what is going on in their lives. The downstairs is filled with their "stuff", but they are not present. The house feels "huge" and very quiet. I miss the chaos and the sounds of young lives. I am grateful that summer is a time to gather at the house again. The girls are in between houses and the boys can work from the house and take vacations.

Of Kurdt's children, I think I know Alex the best and then Reece. The twins, Dominic and Audra are wonderful, but they are generally very quiet, and I don't know them as well. I've lived with Alex for several years when he was a toddler, but I've never lived with Kurdt's other children. We get together occasionally with Kurdt's family, but usually, it is at a family gathering where I seem to spend most of my time catching up on what is happening with the older folks. Kurdt occasionally visits my home and brings Reece, so I get to connect with him. I really enjoy my encounters with the youngest of my grandchildren. He loves science and reading. Dominic and Alex share an apartment and are working and doing very well. Audra is also living on her own and working. All four of the Huige children are loving, caring and hard-working.

During the summer of 2023, Natalie took a semester of study in Italy. She had a great time, and Anthony met up with her at the end of her classes and the two of them traveled around Europe together. They had a wonderful time and saw another world. Summer of 2024, Christina took Spanish classes in Spain, traveled for a week alone, staying in hostels and meeting people from all over the world. She was then joined by both of her brothers to explore Europe. What surprises me is how eagerly the kids welcome adventure and how unafraid they are. They know how to deal with the world and if they are uncertain, they ask questions. I admire how self-assured they are. I traveled when I was young, but I was afraid. I never really felt safe. I'm happy that I did not pass my fear on to them.

Sara and I are basically living alone in the house. We treat each other lovingly and always have done so. We seem to be getting along better and better. I'm thrilled that she is still alive and that the quality of her life is good. It has been more than five years since the doctors thought she had about two months to live. Every day is special to me. The kids have forgiven her for giving up guardianship and seem to understand that her brain tumors probably had a lot to do with the poor judgment she displayed for a period of time before she left for New Mexico. They also seem to have come to terms with her desire to spend her remaining days in the house with television and games. I've given up encouraging her to do something I would define as "meaningful." She is happy doing what she chooses and we are happy with each other. She is doing what she wants and that works for me. She enjoys solitude and I do not. We are definitely different.

Gerry is in assisted living. He can easily carry on a conversation, although the amount of repetition in his speech can drive you crazy. He does not look after himself very well, even with the amount of help available to him. The kids continue to feel burdened by his care. They look after his finances and occasionally clean his room. The floor of his apartment tends to be littered with take-home containers for food, cups, odd pieces of paper and food that happened to fall from the full table. He was an engineer, but his intellectual capacity was damaged by the stroke. He is about as alone as I can imagine a person to be. His choice. He has chosen not to reach out. He seldom answers his phone. He doesn't call his children. He is losing out on life. He still makes no effort to connect in any meaningful way with his children. They have stopped trying with him.

I was just watching the University of Michigan football game with neighbors, and I heard messages coming in on my phone. I got one from Anthony who was returning to his California home but found the time to send me a text of what he had done in New York. I got a picture text from Christina, who was at the game and said hello to me in a picture of herself. I saw a new posting from Alex about a new interest of his. Natalie called and asked if there was a meal tonight. Sara was sitting in the other room watching television and putting up with my chatter with others. It felt absolutely wonderful to feel enveloped in the lives of so many loving people. This is my life now at eighty- four years. I never could have imagined that my life could be this full at this age. I am so fortunate. Life is good.

WE MADE IT

Life goes on. I will forever be grateful that, as a single person, I was able to adopt my children. They have given my life meaning. I can't say that every minute was wonderful, but most moments were memorable, invigorating, and inspiring. There were times when I wondered if I could go on. There were also times when I asked myself, "What have I done? What have I gotten myself into?" In spite of my occasional doubts, I was always able to move ahead. Are there things I would have done differently? You bet there are, but I know that I did my best for them and for me. I know that we love each other. With some issues, particularly relating to politics or religion, we are in different worlds with different languages, realities, facts, and definitely not communicating. I've decided that we do not need to relate on every imaginable level. With Kurdt and his family, I can't discuss religion or politics. I can, however, go to Kurdt's home and the homes of any of my grandchildren and feel loved. I know I belong. I know that my children are in my heart, to stay. I also believe that at some point, we might be able to discuss these touchy topics, or we might decide that we don't have to be able to converse about everything.

Several weeks ago, Kurdt held an outdoor brunch for the family. Sara and I attended. It was held in Kensington Park at Possum Hollow. The day was windy, but absolutely gorgeous. The sun shone brilliantly and we were all grateful for sunglasses. Kelly's parents were present as well as all four of Kurdt and Kelly's children. Audra brought her future in-laws and her fiance to the party. The family is about to grow again, and I can't wait. Next year, Audra will marry Matt and continue her branch of the family. He is a wonderful young man and his parents definitely fit in this growing group. It was a delightful morning and I felt joy belonging to these loving people. We talked and we ate the wonderful food Kurdt and Kelly prepared for us. We fought the wind together and laughed at the puppy trying to catch the napkins and cups falling from the table. We had fun and we are family. This memory would be just a fantasy if I had not adopted Kurdt.

When I debated adopting children, I was clear with myself that my goal was to create a loving family for myself and for the children. I had to ask myself if I, as a single person, had the strength and determination to take on the task of raising two children who had experienced the ravages of war and a great deal of loss. Since I had also experienced violence and war as a child, I thought that my recollections of the past might be helpful in understanding what my children might be dealing with. I also reminded myself that I had spent years as a psychotherapist, and had a treasure trove of information I could turn to relating to childhood trauma. I decided to take on this task, and I have never looked back.

I had no idea how incredible this whole experience would be. I had vulnerable children to think about and I stopped focusing on myself. I felt my world open up as I took on new responsibilities. There were difficult times when injury or sickness threatened our journey, but we managed, with the help of family and friends, to survive and thrive. There were times when I had no idea what to do next or how to solve a problem, so I prayed for a timely resolution to the issue. With patience, the answers came. We made our share of mistakes, but we survived and accepted these mistakes as part of our life experience. It is wonderful to watch my children now raising their own families. I was grateful that I was available for Sara when marital issues drove her from her marital home back to our home.

In 1981 there were three of us who began this journey. There are now thirteen of us, and soon there will be fourteen. When we add extended family, we are a much larger group. For me, this has been the ride of my life. I can't imagine anything being more exciting than having a membership in this cohort. I am grateful that I was given the opportunity to adopt Sara and Kurdt and I appreciate their openness and willingness to share their love with me. Would I do this again? Absolutely! Did the action of adoption change my life? More than anyone can imagine. I am a different person now and I am not alone.

We have all benefited from adoption. The kids are loved and cared for. They were able to leave poverty, violence, and even starvation and legally enter the "land of plenty." They were able to get an education and to marry and have children. They work, they feel good about themselves and they are loving with their children. They both frequently express amazement at how good their lives are at this time. When they visited El Salvador as adults, they got to experience firsthand how far they had come. They were able to connect with people who had been important in their lives pre-adoption. Kurdt was able to give a heartfelt hug to his biological grandmother. Both Sara and Kurdt were able to connect the different parts of their lives to provide closure and bring them peace.

My children got on that plane many years ago because they were told to get on, and they were also told they would have a new "mama" when they landed. There were no guarantees that they would be happy with the decisions made for them. I also had no guarantees that all would work out. They had no information about me or about where they would live. I had very little information about them. We all took a risk and decided to trust. In spite of all of the potential problems, we made it. We learned how to trust one another and build lives together.

Would I do this again? In a heartbeat, I definitely would. I wish there were words that could express how I feel about the creation of this family, but I am speechless.

I love where I am now. I feel so blessed. I am so fortunate.

*Visit 1992 The house I grew
up in Venus is gone replaced
by a clothed Hermes*

The Lokeren house we visited 1992

Kristy, Henriette, Corrie Ria, John, Chris

240

Kristy, Marieke, Ria, Ria, Corrie

Family

My 80th Birthday party 8 grand kids, 2 nieces, 2 nephews Kurdt, Kelly and Sara